Annual Volume One

Selections from the SFWP Quarterly

ISBN 978-1-939650-71-9
ISSN 2573-7422

Published by SFWP
369 Montezuma Ave. #350
Santa Fe, NM 87501
(505) 428-9045
www.sfwp.com

Annual   Volume One

Selections from the SFWP Quarterly

MELANIE J. CORDOVA
Editor of the SFWP Quarterly and the SFWP Annual

ANDREW GIFFORD
Director of the Santa Fe Writers Project

JENNIFER LIU
TERESA STAIANO
Santa Fe Writers Project Interns

Former SFWP Quarterly Editors
K.E. Semmel

From the Editor

This anthology is an exciting new chapter in the life of *The SFWP Quarterly*. In 2002, director Andrew Gifford began the journal's first iteration, publishing almost 400 pieces over the course of thirteen years. On February 1, 2015, editor K.E. Semmel launched the journal in its current form: *The SFWP Quarterly*, dedicated to placing the best fiction and creative nonfiction alongside book reviews, interviews, and articles.

This collection highlights some of our favorite creative pieces since that February launch. I was honored to take the editorial reins from Semmel after issue four and became dedicated to upholding his vision for publishing unique and vibrant pieces from around the world. Today, with the release of this anthology, we at SFWP are doubly focused on that vision.

The stunning works of fiction and creative nonfiction contained in this anthology come from a wide variety of writers, each with her or his own style. These pieces were chosen for their resonance, their ability to follow us around for days after we've read them.

For creative nonfiction, we begin with a modern-day choose-your-own-adventure story by Samantha Edmonds, followed by reflections on space travel by Randon Billings Noble. N. R. Robinson and Morgan Smith each examine psychiatric institutions—one to the north of the Mexican-American border and one to the south. This section ends with a piece by Kayleigh Wanzer on the social and emotional fallout of a pregnancy.

We follow with fiction from Kelli Jo Ford on a young woman's troubled family life, with Sadie Hoagland's period piece on witches and dementia close on her heels. Kerri Pierce provides a countdown to a funeral, Emily Rems contrasts modern attitudes with traditional religious sensibilities, and June Sylvester Saraceno profiles a girl with a BB gun. Atossa Shafaie's piece examines the dark life of a gay man in modern Iran, and Nancy Smith closes out our collection with the end of the world itself.

As thrilled as I am by the depth of these pieces, I am also extremely proud of the number of female voices in this anthology. I hope that readers will be as enthralled from cover to cover as we are.

A special thanks goes to Andrew Gifford, Jennifer Liu, and Teresa Staiano for their efforts in bringing this inaugural anthology together.

Happy reading to you all,
Melanie J. Cordova
October 1, 2017

We want to discover great new work by great new writers and continue the strong, thirteen-year tradition of the original journal and two-year tradition of the SFWP Quarterly. If you have a story to share with us, visit us at sfwp.com.

Contents

Creative Nonfiction

Samantha Edmonds	How to Be	1
Randon Billings Noble	Moon and the Man	3
N. R. Robinson	Our Institutions	9
Morgan Smith	A Member of the Family	21
Kayleigh Wanzer	Thirteen Weeks	31

Fiction

Kelli Jo Ford	Terra Firma	43
Sadie Hoagland	Dementia, 1692	57
Kerri Pierce	Better Than Six	71
Emily Rems	Absolution Bake Shop	79
June Sylvester Saraceno	Buttercup Chain	87
Atossa Shafaie	Wheat to Bread	95
Nancy Smith	Nightfall	107

How to Be

Decide

You're a happy kid. Sit in the back of the church-house three times a week with your feet propped up on the fuzzy red pew in front of you. Wear tights under your scratchy dress—your mother makes you anyway—so that this position is not quite as scandalous. Take off your shoes, black strappy sandals with a silver buckle. Balance a blue three-ring binder on your knees and scribble stories on wide-ruled notebook paper while the preacher shouts, Can I get an Amen? and the congregation says, Glory, Glory. Give these stories titles like "A Dog Called Hope" and "Mad as Heck But Still Best Friends." Declare yourself a writer at the age of ten and show everything you write to your mother as soon as you're finished.

To try something (good lord, anything) else, go to page 77.

To be a writer, jump to page 41.

The Quarterly Issue 1 Spring 2015

Moon and the Man

Everyone asked Neil Armstrong what it was like to walk on the moon. But how did the moon feel?

Four-and-a-half billion years ago the moon formed, the result of a tragic union between the Earth and an unknown, careening planet. Slowly, lento, largo, the Earth pulled itself together and the wreckage of this collision resolved itself into an orbiting moon.

Billions of years later, after the prokaryotes and the eukaryotes, the bilateria and the fish, the insects and seeds and reptiles and mammals, after the birds and the flowers, Homo sapiens evolved. In 35,000 BC, in what is now Swaziland, one of them carved twenty-nine notches into a piece of bone to make the earliest known lunar calendar. Even then we were tracking the moon, measuring it, fixing it. In 1609 an Englishman looked at the moon through a telescope and cut through nearly 239,000 miles of mystery. Maps were made; then globes. In 1839, photographs were taken. We knew what the moon looked like, we had charted all we could see, but what was *there*?

In the English language the moon was masculine until the sixteenth century. Then we remembered Selene, Luna, and Diana and the moon became the passive, feminine reflection of the sun's light, the capacious surface for all our projections, the accommodating repository for our myths and inventions.

*

In 1959 the first man-made object, Luna 2, crash landed on moon. Did the moon feel a difference? Without an atmosphere to protect it, the moon has been bombarded with comets, asteroids, and meteoroids for its entire existence. Without wind or rain to erase and efface, each crater, pit, and pock remains. But perhaps now the moon felt a difference, being hit by something metal and not rock, something systematic, focused, and intentional, something that was not random, but a harbinger.

For millennia the moon's far side was invisible, unknowable, subject only to our speculations: aliens lived there, or ghosts; it was a version of heaven, hell, or purgatory. In 1959 Luna 3 returned the first hazy images of the no-longer-dark side: a rough and barren landscape of crater and shadow.

Then came the Apollo missions, named for the moon's opposite, the god of the sun; the god of music, art, and poetry; the god of knowledge. Apollo's mission was to know the moon, to apprehend it, to master it. A few years before Apollo 11 landed, C.S. Lewis wrote that the moon belonged to all humanity: "he who first reaches it steals something from us all."

When Armstrong's boot hit the surface of the moon in 1969 he stepped into the Mare Tranquilitatis, disturbing its equanimity. For the first time in all its long history a living being walked on the moon. Was there a quiver of longing? A shudder of revulsion? Or just the gray puffs of indifferent dust?

Legend has it that on the moon can be found everything that was wasted on earth: misspent time, squandered wealth, broken vows, unanswered prayers, fruitless tears, unfulfilled desires. What did Neil Armstrong find there? From his life? From mine?

*

Armstrong died when the moon was in its first quarter, on 25 Aug 2012. His ashes—gray as moondust—were buried not in the earth but the sea. His family asked that when you "see the moon smiling down at you, think of Neil Armstrong and give him a wink." A wink is given to indicate that something is a joke or a secret; it can also be a signal of affection or greeting. Does the moon share this jokey affection? Is it smiling—or merely beaming reflected light? Does it feel a sense of loss or is it relieved that that the first man to walk on its surface, to mark it, to leave his tokens and footprints and memory behind, will never return?

The wordless moon has no way of knowing the word "wink" comes from the word "wince."

In September, I drink tea and eat moon cakes, thinking about what I want during the Earth's next orbit around the sun. How do I want to spend my time, what vows will I keep, what desires will I try to fill? What are my fixed relationships and how will I navigate them? What will evolve and what will be ongoing?

But my last prayer is for the moon itself—for it to have what it wants or to be at peace with what it has—silence and sterility while locked into orbit with this blue teeming earth.

How to Be

Rather than

Get accepted into the university of your choice, five and a half hours away from the boy you promised to marry, an hour from your mother. It will take you over two years to get your degree, more if you pursue the PhD, and in that time, he is not willing to relocate to be closer to you. His life has roots, unlike yours.

Leave him. Do not want to, but do it. Cry when you do. Watch him cry, too. Regret it. Think he was good and kind but average. Do not miss him, not at first. There are other boys in your cohort and they have chosen the path you have chosen, the one your ex thinks is crazy, the one made out of words and not tangible things. Perhaps you will fall in love with the words of one of these new men, but maybe not. It doesn't matter. You are here to write.

It is hard. It is, to be honest, mostly miserable. Get a studio apartment to yourself, the first time you have ever lived alone. On weekends, don't leave your apartment. Go two days or more without speaking to another human. Wonder if you exist. Dream of sex, but have none. Drink. Smoke. Spend your money on those vices instead of groceries. Miss your mother. Start to even miss, much later, the golden-eyed boy you've left behind. Wonder if you have made the wrong choice.

Start forgetting to call your mother every day. Settle on every other, then once a week. Then every two. Run out of things to say to her when she starts calling you. She does not know the names of your new grad student friends. She does not know what you're working on or what your apartment looks like.

Go out on weekdays with the students in your cohort and order PBRs and talk about Don DeLillo and David Foster Wallace in smoky bars with no windows. Is the Mona Lisa just like the Most Photographed Barn in America? Will post-postmodernism ever catch on? Bring work home with you. Greet in the office on Monday the same people you shared Saturday night with. Write. Write. Write. Find in this terrible sadness some reluctant joy, surrounded by people who think like you, write like you. These peers will call your work prolific, but you will just call it lonely.

Wonder what your mother would think of it.

To give it all up, to move back and *call home*, go to page 69.

To keep following the words even into the darkest *void*, go to page 55.

The Quarterly Issue 6 Summer 2016

Our Institutions

Imagine Nichols Avenue, because Nichols is where we are headed. Granddad Alvarez does not take the usual Sunday scenic route: through downtown D.C., past the Lyndon B. Johnson White House and the sunburnt, sign-shaking Vietnam protesters. Instead, we hook a right from Randolph Place, and head down straight North Capital Street, past groups of Negroes huddled around bus stops and streaming from Catholic and Baptist and AME churches. My seven-year-old sister, Cookie, stares out at the hubbub. Because nothing will hold still in my nine-year-old head, I clench my eyes and study the glowing red of my inner eyelids.

It is 1965 and Gemini 5 is orbiting the planet. It has been two years since Cookie and I came to rest in the welter of the Alvarez home, a place where days are so unpredictable and like any other that time seems to stand stock-still. Two years since seeing hard-mouthed Grandma rheumy-eyed and wailing, "Lord ha' mercy, they done killed our President!" And TV images of a white man's head jerking under a halo of flesh-and-blood mist as his pink-suited companion scrambles over the trunk of their long black convertible. Two years earlier, Grandma signed Mama over to Saint E's, the city's government-run loony bin. To be fair to Grandma, Mama was on to her fourth suicide attempt.

This trip to see Mama, like our first trip two years past, is sometime after Halloween but before New Year's Day. We rumble down into the New Jersey Avenue tunnel, up onto the Southeast Freeway, over the 11th Street Bridge, and into the rising stench of the snot-green Anacostia River. Braking hard into the first exit, we descend onto Nichols Avenue. My anxiety builds through the slow climb up the gradual hill. Where Nichols levels out, a twelve-foot high brick wall ribbons the right of the avenue as far as I can see. We turn into the second gated entrance. Beside the elfin slit-window set into the stone of the guardhouse, a weathered bronze plaque announces: "Saint Elizabeth's Hospital est. 1855."

The Oz-like vista no longer surprises me. I could have sworn, back on our first visit, that we were entering some hidden-away fairy town, with ancient street signs set into winding roads leading to dozens of diminutive castles, and small groups strolling paths carved into the snowy slopes of a postage stamp village with a hilltop view of D.C.'s historic skyline.

On that first visit, Grandma mused, "Way back when, Saint E's was called The Government Hospital for th' Insane. Yo' Mama's docta' said it was th' world's first and largest asylum. Over a hundred thousand been locked away hea'—all types of crazy I neva' heard of." Grandma's minimus moved across the pamphlet: "Manic-depressive an' phobics; psychotics, paranoid *an'* schizophrenic; dis-so-ci-a-tive sickness," she sounded out, "amnesia an' multiple personalities; delirium an' dementia."

"What kinda' sick is Mama?" I asked, fear under my affected carelessness.

Following her own thoughts, Grandma said, "The docta's give 'em counsel'n.' But, if you ask me, ain't no way to fix 'em." She told us, "He said they can't get enough nurses or' docta's. Must be why them nutjobs is all nasty and beat up th' way they is."

Unwinding that first visit in my mind, I marched up the snow-covered walkway, my rubber-soled sneakers slipping on the slick sidewalk as I examined Mama's new home. Like many of Saint

Elizabeth's buildings, hers was red brick stacked gothic style. As if some fantastic fortress, the structure had a tall center turret sandwiched between two smaller towers with crenellations along the top. In the keep-like lobby, a guard looked up from his *Jet Magazine*. After registering our names, he grunted into a black rotary handset and then pointed without looking at an ancient elevator. We jerked and rattled to our destination floor, and then spilled into a cube of a hallway. A small wall sign read: "Ward 3." Granddad pushed the single button set into the frame of the windowless door and we waited.

As Cookie squeezes my hand this day, I fidget alongside Granddad, standing stiff before that same windowless door. Grandma mutters, "Don' know why dese people always take so damn long!"

My stomach churns at the now-familiar fecal odor mixed with the smell of urine and Pine-Sol, a biotic stink that creeps beneath the door along with screams and the manic laughter that never fails to whip up fear within me: fear that whatever has touched Mama is budding within me; fear of being consigned to St. E's and locked in a ward like this.

Mama's mental illness, as I have experienced it, blossoms from a kind of unwilling hysteria. Because a feeling is a feeling (that cannot be reasoned with), I have decided that my own path to sanity is unemotion. I have deduced that strong-mindedness—control over anger, sadness, and, yes, fear—is the key to mental health. So I maintain my façade of calm through the clanking of the lock turning and the heavy door swinging open.

The four of us push through the Babel of voices into the now-expected semicircle of residents swarming like an audience settling in to watch some unintentional theater; faces expressionless, or twisting in laughter and sorrow; old, young, male, female, Negroes, and Caucasians all sporting the standard getup of pale green hospital gowns with tie-strings dangling over exposed buttocks.

Back on that first visit, half-circled by the residents as we are this day, I watched as a thin big-jointed man with *Orderly In Charge* sewn across the breast of his white jacket shooed the half-circle, "Get on now! Go on back to your bus'ness or you ain't getting no cigarettes."

We stood in the same cavernous room. To the front and right of the room sat then, like now, a chest-high counter behind which the two other white-jackets casually lounged. The very casualness of those uniformed men in that chaotic setting exuded a certain authority, a sense of inevitability. The nearest white-jacket nodded toward a corner where sunlight pushing through a barred window illuminated a ratty brown davenport and matching easy chair. That part of the room lay at the end of a long hallway punched with cave-like doorways. It was from one of these doorways that Mama emerged.

Before that first visit to Saint Elizabeth's, Cookie and I had gotten no news of Mama for months, since before her last self-destructive compulsion. Whenever we asked, Grandma'd said, "Y'all 'a find out soon enuf." But *soon enuf* never showed up. During those news-less months after Mama's disappearance, we'd been inconsolable: Cookie's face leaking tears and emitting a nonstop sibilance; me, withholding my emotions until bedtime when I'd wept then slept and, more often than not, pissed into my thin hard mattress; mornings awakened by cold urine-soaked sheets, a hurried stripping and flipping of the gray-striped pallet, then lugging my mess down to the basement washroom as Grandma followed, "You fucked up my good mattress n' sheets." I'd sent out psychic messages. Even, at times, cried out, "Come back, Mama!" But, it was Grandma who'd inevitably answered from her sofa-in-state, "Shut that racket, boy!" Living under Grandma's thumb took concentration and an odd sort of *non*control, a kind of surrender, so that the hurt zipped right through, leaving no damage at all. This, at least, is what I believed then.

On that first visit to Saint E's, mitigating my enthusiasm was the fact that I had no idea what to expect. The very air stood at attention that day. When Mama emerged from one of the cavernous doorways, the in-charge orderly guided her. Knobby fingers encircling Mama's pale-slender arm, he whispered what I imagined were encouragements as she shuffled toward us in a gait different from the light prance we'd known. Her chestnut hair was electric, her pale skin paler. A hospital gown hung from her thinner-than-usual frame. Most noticeably, Mama's typically animated façade was as expressionless as the face on a nickel. Incredibly—incredible because it's difficult to convey how this could be true—Mama was still beautiful.

What was beautiful about Mama on that first visit was the stately manner with which she tried to right herself when she stumbled, and how she struggled to keep her sagging head erect, the slipping gown on her still-elegant shoulders, the feeble but dignified attempts she made to shrug out of the orderly's grasp. Mama was beautiful in the instinctive way that she, in spite of the circumstances, tried to maintain dignity and a sense of independence.

"Mad'line, you be good," the orderly said with a plugged-in sort of grin. "I'll be back ta get you in a few." He winked familiarly at her, then us, before turning and joining the other white-jackets chatting it up back at the nurse-less nurse's station.

Cookie threw her head and shoulders into Mama's lap. "Mommy!"

Grandma trilled, "Cheechee, why yo' walkin' round hea half-naked like yo' ain' got no home trainin'?"

During the orderly's instructions on that first visit, Cookie's hugging and crying, and Grandma's chiding, Mama sat immobile and placid, as if an invisible membrane sheltered her from the surrounding chaos. Perched at the edge of the easy chair, I watched, torn between wanting to run away from Mama and needing to bury my face between the bumps of her small breasts. Just then Mama looked up; her eyes locked with mine. Even in their dull emptiness, they were the eyes I'd always known. Her contrite-but-porcelain gaze shifted down to where Cookie clutched at her gown. "Hi, babies," Mama muttered in a soft, garbled voice.

Since that first visit, we have visited Saint E's a dozen times. Before the first visit, I had barely contained my excitement. Afterwards, I visited reluctantly. When visiting day approached, anxiety built, through the weekend and during those scenic Sunday drives. By the time we topped the crest and at sight of the walls, my apprehension was unbearable.

The Mama who emerges from the doorway on this visit seems abruptly changed: a sudden and imperfect improvisation of Mama. She walks alone. Plump all over—her face swollen, arms and legs dimpled, belly distended—she grins wide when she sees us. Why, I wonder, hasn't Mama wiped the rivulets of sweat from her forehead, and from the short dark hairs growing above her lip? When Mama squeezes me tight, stink rises, hot, from her armpits.

My life is like that. That is to say, I never seem to catch anyone or anything changing. The universe seems to barely move forward. Time and change are costive, practically invisible. When change does manifest itself, it is a magical phenomenon, like the growth of grass, unseen until the day it is irrefutable.

Mama's hair is disheveled, but when she looks at me, her eyes are clear. "My baby," she cackles, then pulls me close. As Cookie tearfully hugs what is left of her, Mama announces to the residents clotting around us, "Everybody, this hea's my son Nicky. Ain't he a doll?"

Cookie's face, inches below mine, is scarlet with love. Forever, it seems, Cookie and I have lapped Mama's devotion like rich cream. This day, I burn with humiliation. I feel the weight of my mother's insanity: our no-longer-shocked-treated Mama at home in the ward, speaking to the crazies as if they are real people—as if they are extended family at a backyard barbecue or cheerful neighbors dropping by. I can hear the orderlies chortling. Their laughter is a hammer. I can feel a pounding swell at the front of my brain. I pull from Mama's grasp, and out and away from the swarm.

"Grandma, can I wait downstai's?"

"Wha's wrong wit' yo', boy? Go be wit yo' mama."

I glance back. Mama is busy introducing Cookie to one of the group. "—And this hea's Mister Ford, my soon-ta-be husban'." As the vacant-eyed, giant of a man she is presenting stares off into space, Mama throws back her auburn-curls and brays a wild laugh. I can see silver-gray molars and the pink fleshy teardrop at the back of her throat.

I turn away—shoulders hunched, eyes to the ground—mortified that Mama is locked away in this place and living under these conditions. I burn at the sight of her, treated like a madwoman by people who know about these sorts of things, and at the prospect of these people seeing me the same way. How can she, I think, do this to herself, and to us? How could she have tried to die?

"She didn' mean it," Cookie says, as if her thoughts run along identical lines. Cookie can always read my expressions, can almost read my mind. She still believes in Mama. Two years older and wiser, I know better.

That great eccentric, Time, I will discover, is not only coincident with change, it's the active event of change, some thing that can be stretched: sped up or shortened when filled with the new or interesting, slowed or lengthened by monotony or emptiness. If it had been possible to manipulate time, time control is the magic wand I would have waved as a child.

Over the past two years of living with the Alvarezes, time has seemed inert, with days like weeks, weeks like months, one month of soaring routine, repetition, disorder, inconsequence, and angst identical to the next. It has been an utterly banausic—to the point of drudgery—period when my need for Mama morphed into sudden tantrums, fist fights with schoolmates, a sullen silence my response to the nuns' reprimands. Then, abruptly expelled, kicked out of Saint Martin's Elementary, where I have learned I can gobble a page, a figure, a rule, consume whole chapters in a fraction of the time it takes my classmates, a place I have been appreciated, and that I have come to appreciate.

I told myself that getting kicked out of school did not matter. But it mattered to Grandma. She threatened for weeks: "I'm done wit' y'all monkeys. Let the orphanage deal wit' yur mess!" I did not plead for forgiveness as I had before. Over the years, I've come to believe that niggles and threats are Grandma's way. I am changing, I feel, morphing into a newer, wiser Nick. It is grass-growing sort of change. No longer a naïf of seven, at nine I know what is what. At nine, I know the meaning of suicide.

"She didn' actually *d-d-do it*," Cookie stammers.

And I know death. The way I figure, suicide is not rocket science; you either do it or you do not. Because of luck or circumstance or ineptitude, Mama has not been successful courting death. But what if she had been?

I see dead animals all the time. Stray dogs and rats flattened like pancakes on D.C. streets, lying lifelessly, regarding the round world one-dimensionally, their innards splattered, a star-spangled declaration of death. Even cats, with their supposed nine lives, are merely mortal.

I recall watching a group of young ragamuffins catch an alley cat and tie it in a burlap sack. Just for the fun of it, it seemed, they set the sack on fire. The cat—writhing, keening, indefatigably alive—fought violently to escape the fiery trap until, at some interminable point, the bag lay still. After those boys danced away hooting and elbowing one other, I examined the sack and the cat up close. There was zero, zippo, *nada* spiritual about death, I concluded. Death is the opposite of religious, a thing secular and nothing more, almost indecent in its profane physicality.

I wonder why Mama did not do what that cat and all the lowliest creatures of the planet do everyday—fight to live.

Cookie stutters, "M-M-Mama's gettin' betta'. Sh-She ain' gonna try agin."

Mama is worse. She has tried to die more than once and *will* try again. During our Sunday drives, I wonder when it was that Mama decided to leave her troubles—and us—for someone else to confront and resolve. I wonder why Mama's will to live has gone. Maybe someone snatched it away.

"Daddy beat her too bad," Cookie offered.

But Mama never tried to fight back. Not with Dad, not with Grandma. Even after deciding to kill herself, Mama never faced down death. She is no hero: she never stood in front of a train or jumped from a tall building. She tried to lure Death to her by swallowing a bottle of prescription pills, and then lay unconscious waiting for Him to strike.

I blame Mama for the stain of sadness that has spread through our lives. She hurt Cookie more than me, is what I tell myself. I have watched Cookie's limitless energy dissipate, hear the fluctuant stutter she has acquired. Cookie, since our first visit to Saint E's, has grown desperate for Mama, like a junky keening for the next fix. I've promised myself that I'll never be so needy, not for Mama, not for anyone.

The adult Nick will become aware of the battles that raged within on those Sunday drives, clashes between his anger with Mama and his love for her. That he fought against love, fought and thought rather than felt that Mama was a coward. As an adult, I will acknowledge that I wished, at times, that Mama had been successful when she'd tried to kill herself.

"Ma-Mama loves us," Cookie says. "She loves you more than me."

I do not love Mama, not anymore. That's what I told myself then. What was true is that I *had* not loved her. And because I was fearful of Mama dying, I wanted death and its uncertainty pinned down, rather than drifting loose, like a lost balloon, liable to pop up anytime, anywhere. Looking back, I wanted to put distance between Mama and me.

On that first visit to Saint E's, I never cried. Seeing Mama drugged and, as we later learned, electric shock-treated, somehow numbed me, too. Still, I was relieved on that first visit when our allotted thirty minutes with Mama expired.

As the orderly in charge vectored away from the counter and toward us, my still-beautiful Mama looked up and mumbled something.

"What you say Mad'line? I didn't hear you," the orderly said.

Mama repeated herself, in a low garbled voice, "Excuse me, sir. Did you take yo' turn wit' me yet?" At Mama's question, an unnatural quietness seemed to descend upon the room, the ward's whole voltage changed.

The orderly, laughing nervously, said, "Mad'line, what you talkin' about?"

"You know."

"Why you gonna ask me somethin' like that?" said the orderly, looking around at us, shoulders shrugging as if to say, "Ain't she crazy?" as if he wanted to beat the idea of Mama's craziness upside our heads. "Mad'line, you gonna give folks the wrong idea."

Granddad and Grandma stared, puzzled, then embarrassed-looking. They never uttered a word.

"What?" I asked, elbowing Cookie.

"What?" Cookie said to me.

Lips pressed together in a white-lipped smile, the orderly hurriedly pulled Mama to her feet, and then he half-walked, half-dragged her down the darkened hall.

How to Be

A normal life

Finish your career as an undergrad. Expect an engagement ring for a graduation present. You are not mistaken. Pretend not to know what's happening when the golden-eyed boy takes you to a fancy restaurant, the one in the city that overlooks the river. When he gets down on one knee, put your hands on your chest. Cry when he asks you. Kiss him on the mouth, like you have done hundreds of times. Following this path, you will never kiss any mouth but this one, not ever.

Frame your creative writing degree and put it on the wall. Half-heartedly write stories but never submit them to magazines. The golden-eyed boy is supportive but doesn't ask to read anything you write. This is fine because you will never finish anything you start. Your mother is still your biggest fan. She will be your only reader but she will be proud. She will begin to ask about what's next—jobs, money, mortgages, that's what she believes makes a good life. Let writing become a hobby.

Plan your wedding with the golden-eyed boy and the rest of your life, too. Save yourself and your virginity for marriage. Ask him to stop drinking. On both accounts, he won't mind. He is so happy to be with you, he will do anything you want, except stay in the city where you were born. He has a job and a home up north and has carved a spot for you in the life he has built. You are welcome to it. You are small;

you can fit into the space he has made for you. Your mother will cry every time she thinks about you moving more than half an hour away.

You are twenty-one years old. Hesitate. Think to yourself, what else can you do with a BA in English?

To accept the life he is offering and make it work *with work*, go to page 85.

To go to grad school close to home *rather than* be his, jump to page 7.

The Quarterly Issue 7 Fall 2016

A Member of the Family

I hear a strange clicking sound, look down the semi-dark corridor, and see a shadowy figure near the second of the two cells. A man is holding what looks like an old coffee can in his left hand. When he withdraws his right hand from the can, I see that it's Cholo, one of the more dangerous mental patients, and he has a blue plastic Gillette razor.

Then Cholo leans forward and reaches through the bars with the razor. He's shaving someone inside the cell; the clicking sound was him swishing the razor around in the water in the coffee can to clean it.

Holding my camera, I edge closer. This is my job—to tell the story of these patients, the men and women whom Pastor José Antonio Galván, the founder of this mental asylum in the desert west of Juárez, Mexico, calls his *loquitos*, or little crazy ones.

Inside the cell, a lean, dark-haired man stands passively, his face soaped up. The only sound is the scraping of the razor as Cholo gently shaves him. Neither man pays any attention to me and my camera. Then the blankets on the floor of the cell begin to twist and move as if there's an animal or snake underneath. I jump back but it's only two more patients who have been sleeping. They stand up to await their turn.

This is Friday, shaving day. Every one of Pastor's one hundred *loquitos* will be bathed and cleaned up. These are people he has rescued from the brutal streets of Juárez, protecting them from being killed by the *sicarios*, or gunmen, as well as the police and soldiers who are often just as deadly. Many are addicts, many have been recently deported, a number of them have committed murders, others seem to be chronically brain damaged. Galván doesn't care what their backgrounds are; he believes that they all have potential, that they are *tesoros escondidos*, or hidden treasures. He is giving them dignity as well as food, shelter and safety and a sense of family and caring.

As for me, I'm a retired lawyer who writes and photographs for a scattering of newspapers throughout the Southwest. I began this border project several years ago with the idea of making monthly trips to every border town from the Pacific coast on the west to the Gulf of Mexico on the east. I traveled to Palomas, Sasabe, Naco, Agua Prieta, Sonoyta, Tijuana. Finally, overcoming my own fears, I began to visit Juárez, which was then the most dangerous city in the world. I visited a rehab center for young women, an orphanage for the badly damaged infants of Tarahumara Indians, a food bank in the Colonia 16 de Septiembre that is maintained by Catholic volunteers from El Paso, a local jail, a public mental hospital, and a Christmas gift program that took me southwest to Asención. I also helped build houses near the border with two different U.S. groups, one from Santa Fe where I live. There's a hidden world here of volunteers—Mexican and American— who provide the human services that the Mexican government has ignored. They often work under very dangerous circumstances. I became so attached to these people that, rather than trying to go from one coast to the other as originally planned, I began to make repeat visits to Palomas, Juárez, and this mental asylum in particular.

Cholo rinses the razor, puts the coffee can down, and reaches through the bars again. With his left hand, he holds the man's right ear and steadies his face while he carefully shaves his cheek. Then he pulls out a wet rag and wipes the rest of the soap off the man's face. A stocky, powerful young man who hears voices, he's one of the few patients who scares me, yet he is caring for another patient with an astonishing gentleness.

When I return to the patio where the majority of the patients spend their days, breakfast has just been served and several patients are collecting the trays and taking them into the desert behind the building where another crew washes them. I had arrived just after dawn, crossing the border at Santa Teresa west of Juárez and El Paso, hoping that the Mexican soldiers wouldn't check the boxes of used clothing, candy, and cigarettes in my car and then either confiscate them or take me into custody. What had surprised me—because I had never arrived at the asylum this early—was to see so many patients at work. Whether it was collecting firewood in the desert, building a fire under the huge barrel of water outside so that there would be boiling water for washing the trays, chopping vegetables in the kitchen, or washing clothing and blankets, many of the patients have assignments and they just get up and do them. To Galván, this is crucial. Working, producing, having a role in the running of the facility—all of this leads, he believes, to a sense of dignity and usefulness that is therapeutic.

I had also driven to the shack where Elvira, the cook and her two grandkids, Hector (15) and Yeira (14), lived. They needed a ride to the asylum. As a grandfather myself, it's hard to imagine having my grandchildren spend their weekends in a mental asylum, but what else can Elvira do? Her son abandoned the two kids, she has to work on weekends, and it's not safe for them to be alone in their neighborhood. When I first met them, they were mixing with the patients in the patio so I assumed that they too were patients. Now they're helping me with my photography projects. I photograph patients; Hector and Yeira write down their names and other basic data. Then we hand out candy and cigarettes. This may seem like a tiny reward—one candy bar and a cigarette—but it's a break in the monotony of the ample but bland food, something to look forward to and a sign that an outsider cares about them. (I come at least once a month without fail.) Unless you actually see the reactions on the faces of the patients, it's hard to understand the enormous pleasure that these tiny gestures bring them. Hector and Yeira also watch out for me. When I was photographing a man in one cell, a man named Victoriano reached out from another cell and pickpocketed me. Hector caught him and made him return my papers.

In return, I either take them to the *segunda*, or flea market, and buy them clothing or pay Elvira directly. This fall, I'll pay for the band at Yeira's *quinceañera*, or fifteenth birthday party, a crucially important event in the life of a young Mexican woman. She is exactly two weeks younger than my oldest granddaughter but their lives are as different as if one were living on the moon and the other on Mars.

Once they interviewed patients when I wasn't there, one of whom, Arón, had killed at least fifteen people. I was stunned.

"Weren't you upset when he described these killings?" I asked Yeira.

"No." She shook her head stoically. "But he was crying."

Although Elvira is the boss of this simple little kitchen (her primitive two-burner stove has to turn out three hundred meals a day), her kitchen crew begins work well before her arrival. They may be *loquitos*, but when the sun begins to rise, they simply get up and go to work. Although Pastor Galván has only two employees who are not also mental patients, most American companies would give anything to have a workforce this reliable.

The patio where most spend their days is a rectangular space perhaps 150 feet long and 50 feet wide. At the west end there is a sliding gate that opens up to the parking area and the desert. At the east end, there are large rooms on each corner, one for the men and one for the women. The women have beds or cots; the men sleep on mats on the floor. Along the center wall, there are more cells for the permanently dangerous, for new arrivals whose behavior might be unknown, and for people who have suffered bipolar breaks or eruptions and have to be restrained temporarily until they calm down.

Each time I visit the mix has changed. The wiry, handsome Jaime will be in a cell one month, and then for three or more months he is one of the best kitchen workers. Becky, for whom I bring the cigarettes because she killed another woman in an argument over a cigarette, is generally a calming influence in the patio. (I'm a life-long non-smoker but when I heard her story, I decided to be safe and bring her cigarettes. Then I saw how much pleasure one cigarette could give these patients.) Unfortunately she too has bi-polar eruptions and has to be put in a cell.

"You know about mental hospitals, don't you?" Dr. Pantoja, the visiting psychiatrist, asks me. He comes out every Sunday morning for which Galván pays him $50 when he has the money.

After law school, I had been the Public Defender of Adams County, Colorado; part of my job was to act as the guardian ad litem for all of the county residents who had been detained on mental health holds. So I've spent hundreds of hours with mental patients as well as with defendants in criminal cases.

"Once I went to visit a patient in the Colorado State Hospital in Pueblo," I answer. "The guards let me into the ward where all the patients spent their days and then they forgot about me. I was locked inside for hours."

Pantoja tries to control his laughter. He also works in the *cereso*, or municipal jail, one of the most dangerous jobs in Juárez. Seventeen inmates were killed in a recent riot there. He and Galván both live under threat, whether from killers who try to extort them or the police who are just as frightening. It's hard, therefore, for me to allow myself to feel afraid during these one- or two-day-a-month visits when this is something they live with every day.

In the center of the patio sits a large white enamel tub half full of water where blankets have been dumped for their weekly washing. One patient, wearing rubber boots, is stomping on them to work the dirt loose. Others carry buckets of water in from a tap outside. Soon they will lift the heavy, wet plaid blankets out of the tub, dump the dirty water out, pour in fresh water, add soap, and do the stomping again. Then they'll take the blankets out a second time. A patient will hold each end of each blanket and they'll twist it and squeeze out the water. Finally the blankets will be loaded in a wheelbarrow and wheeled out to the rear of the building to be hung on a long clothesline or draped over mesquite bushes to dry.

Now Cholo is back in the patio, shaving an older man who is blind in one eye. A big, powerful-looking patient named Benito is trimming the toenails of an older woman in a wheelchair. Two tiny sisters, Elia and Leticia, are seated in a shady area. It looks like Elia is combing Leticia's hair.

Dr. Pantoja grips my arm. "You saw what happened when I walked in this morning. They all yelled my name and came over to hug me. You can't do that in your country. Hug patients. Show that kind of emotion. You can't have patients shaving each other, trimming toenails." He waved at the two sisters, Elia and Leticia. "They can't talk coherently but somehow they know how to cheer the other patients up."

He points to the room where the medications are kept. "Imagine this. The medications are dispersed by Josué, a former addict. He spent ten years in prison in California before they deported him."

When we sit at the small table in the kitchen, Galván grabs Pantoja's arm and tells him that a police patrol has just called and they are bringing a new patient, a woman named Marta.

"We know nothing about her."

"It doesn't matter, Pastor. If the police say take her, you take her. You just do what they say. It's a tiny price to pay for keeping the police happy," Pantoja answers.

Galván is angry. The goal is to run the asylum as a real hospital where people are taken in for legitimate medical reasons, not just because the police are, in essence, doing a "street sweeping." But this is Juárez and Pantoja is right. With the police, there's no room for bargaining or equivocation.

Then we hear the vehicles arriving outside; the engines have a heavy, oppressive sound. Two police cars have stopped in the desert at the edge of the building and a number of officers are getting out. Most have automatic weapons. Three of them are pulling on the arms of a burly, ragged-looking woman. Her clothes are torn and she had no pants, just underwear. Her hair is matted.

"This is Marta," Pantoja whispers to Galván as an officer approaches with papers for him to sign.

Then Pantoja turns to me and says, "We have to care for her but we get no money, nothing to cover her costs. We get no real diagnosis so we don't really know what's wrong." Then he shrugs. "*Así es México.*" "That's Mexico."

I wait outside with the officers as several patients take Marta's arms and lead her inside. Chatting with the man who looks like the leader, I think that maybe I can get him to let me photograph them with their automatic weapons, the desert in the background. One of the officers takes the clip out of his pistol and re-inserts it over and over with a harsh clicking sound. Pantoja has retreated to the gate and calls for me to follow him but I feel that I have to get the picture. Then another officer steps behind me; I can feel his breath on my neck. Pantoja returns, grips my arm, yanks me toward the patio.

"Don't be crazy. Get in here. It's not safe with them," he whispers in a strained voice. We are both pouring sweat as we lean against the inner wall of the patio and catch our breath.

Then I see a new Marta. The other patients have bathed her and given her a clean smock. Her head has been shaved and the filthy matted hair is gone. Benito is trimming her fingernails as Elia and

Leticia gently hold her arms. With her round, bullet head and tattoos on her thick, powerful arms, she looks like a linebacker. I wonder what she has done. Killed someone as Becky did? The relative calm of this place obscures the fact that many of these patients have killed. You just don't imagine it until you hear their stories.

Then Benito says something about her toenails and I look down. Her feet are bloody and the toenails ragged and infected looking. As he reaches down to her feet, she lets out a shriek, breaks loose and runs across the patio. The other patients dart away from her.

"Let her be," Galván shouts. "Let her calm down."

We stand and watch, Galván, Pantoja, Benito, Cholo who is still holding the coffee can and razor, the two sisters, some forty other patients. No one knows what to do. Finally Elia and Leticia walk quietly over to her and sit on the cement bench, one on either side. The patio is silent. Marta is big enough to crush both women. Elia puts her arm on Marta's shoulder, carefully leans toward the agitated woman and rests her cheek on her shoulder. Marta has her hands over her face. All we can see are her freshly trimmed fingernails.

Leticia rests her head on Marta's other shoulder. I have no idea how long they remain that way. It seems like forever as we watch nervously. Finally Marta takes her hands away from the front of her face, revealing herself, revealing a smile.

"Now she's a member of the family," Pantoja whispers. "Now she's a member of the family."

How to Be

To fill

Fall in love with a boy with golden eyes your freshman year at university. He is patient, notices you first, and thinks you're worth the wait. Don't sleep with him. Unless you are fighting, which you rarely ever do, never write about him. He is good and kind. You are happy. Sacrifice being a writer in exchange for being his.

You've never had a boyfriend before him. He is your first date and your first hand-hold and your first *I think you're beautiful* and your first kiss and your first penis and your first almost everything. You want to be his last all of these things.

Unintentionally start to forget you were meant to be a writer.

Much later, before graduation, quite by accident, start to fall in love with someone else. He is a writer like you. He is older. Call him the stranger, even after he isn't one. Consider leaving the golden-eyed boy and never looking back, not even on paper. The stranger makes you write like you haven't since you were fifteen years old writing poetry about how much you loooooved Teen Dream in a Boy Band, the one you thought you'd marry someday. Don't tell your mother about the stranger. Write new stories, the only different ones since you came to college. Feel special, feel free, for the first time. Make a choice.

To stay with the first boy, even if it means never picking up a pen again, choose *a normal life*, and go to page 19.

To be wooed by this dark and handsome stranger *with words*, jump to page 93.

The Quarterly Issue 6 Summer 2016

Thirteen Weeks

1.

I'm not eating again. Not because I don't want to, but because it's making me sick again. And my limbs feel like sand again, feel like hanging on the ends of puppet strings except no one is pulling them. That's the problem: he's not pulling them. So I wake up, swollen eyes and head aching and the sun isn't out. It's warm for December but I'm freezing.

It's like this: The less you eat the less you sleep the easier you bruise the easier you freeze.

I wake up crying again because last night he told me that he loves me but he needs time. Because he wants a future that he can't see right now. And I think of fog, think of rain, think of ice, think of how slippery it will be if the warm air keeps up. I walk into work and everyone says: *You look awful.* It's been forty-eight hours but I keep having to sneak into the storage room to cry. *This isn't like me*, I hear myself say to a co-worker and she just replies: *I'm sure he'll come back, I'm sure you'll come back from this.*

So I call him, tell him I have to see him. He says that isn't a good idea. Except that later I ride in a cab past him, he's outside of the neighborhood bar. And he's smoking, he's talking, he's moving his hands erratically. I tell the driver *let me out here*, but what I really mean is *get me out of here*, and I fall down on the sidewalk, screaming, hoping he can hear me, come to his senses. But he doesn't and he won't, so

I'm still not eating. Three bites of a soft pretzel yesterday but I haven't been eating. Couldn't make myself swallow it. Spit it back up into my shaking hands in the break room at work. Covered in saliva, barely chewed. The back of my throat tastes like burning, and nothing wants to stay down, anyway.

Still, some of me thinks: disappearance.

Thinks: invisibility. Thinks: *if he won't love me I will be so quiet, he won't hear me at all, no one will see me.*

And I stare out of my living room window, wondering if he'll walk past on his walk to work, wondering if it will ever get cold enough to snow.

2.

December disappears and suddenly, January. It's the second week of temperatures so cold snow can't even form. I can see my breath in my bedroom. There are tiny circle dots of frost on the inside of my windows. Two days ago he came over and said the break was now permanent, said: *I don't love you now, I'm not sure I ever loved you then.* The fact that we are neighbors—something that seemed so convenient and so much like oh if I believed in fate—now feels as sharp as the cold air across my face. One day ago he walked past me as I was taking out the trash and I felt the rage boil over uncontrollably, I yelled *go fuck yourself* to his back. He never turned around. He just kept walking.

It all feels the worst in the morning. After the nights of two Xanax, three glasses of wine, and all of it on an empty stomach. I sit with my back against the cold bathtub, shivering, taking in deep breaths, dry heaving. There's not even bile, but the muscle movement of coughing makes me feel better. My roommate asks, after the fifth day of this, in her broken English: *Is it all okay?* I don't know what to say.

I put on two pairs of pants, a big pair of boots, walk up the street to buy some lentil soup. I see him walking toward me but he turns, takes a different way back to his house. I probably look terrible, anyway.

My roommate says: *It's cold out*, and I nod. *I bought some soup*, I reply. Stir the spoon through it. Eat four bites, slow, slurping, feel the way it goes down my throat. Rip off a piece of bread. Chew five times and spit it out: a tiny ball of soup-soaked bread, half-eaten, undigested. Put it in the fridge. Throw it away in six days.

3.

No one wants to be around you, my friend is yelling, as we're standing outside of his apartment. It's not important that it's also my ex's apartment, that the friend is also his best friend. And I'm crying. And I don't want him to see that I'm crying, but I'm crying. I'm crying too much these days. *I'm sorry*, I say, but it's sloppy, slobbery, meaningless, because I'm sobbing.

You're letting this define you, he says.

I'm trying, you say. *I really, really am trying.*

You're indulging, he says back, almost spitting. Looking at me like I'm repulsive, letting me know that I am disgusting.

You're wallowing.

But still, in spite of myself, I am starting not to miss him. At least, not in a way that feels so tangible. Not in any way that I can hold on to.

4.

feel a burning in the back of your throat,
feel it travel
toward the center of your chest.
taste acid.
heartburn.
take a sip of beer.
feel dizzy, nauseous.
feel bloated, gigantic, feel like someone
could probably pop you.

but then sometimes you are a deflated balloon.

lately. a pile of rocks.

and this sickness is getting worse.

put your beer down on the bar,

give a quiet goodbye,

go home, throw up five times.

5.

I will know before it is confirmed. I will predict the bruising and
the scar. Before I slip on ice in the middle of the street, even though
almost-March should be too late for all of this snow, for so much ice,
I will wonder if spring will ever come, and I will know, I will know. I
will know before I get home and lift up the leg of my gray sweatpants,
before I wipe away the gravel, before I wince at how it stings. When I
apply pressure, before I close my eyes: the first time I've seen blood in
months and I will know, I will know before it is confirmed.

Did you shake, did you stutter, could you cry at all?

Think of your mother, how she must have looked upon learning of your
arrival.

I call Planned Parenthood twenty minutes after, still clutching
the test in my sweaty palm. I hide it in the corner of my bedroom,
feel like I need to keep it for some reason, that purple positive glaring
at me from across the room. I call Planned Parenthood, but it's been
too long, and I can't tell them the exact date of my last period, and
I whisper that maybe it was three months ago, try to tell them that
I haven't been sleeping or eating, and they say they can't see me. It's
been too long and they can't see me.

The private doctor's office can fit me in two weeks from tomorrow.
The receptionist tells me they will call me the day before. "I just,"
I stop, unsure of what to say. "Am I allowed to just pretend it's not
happening while I wait?"

I go out to lunch with a friend three hours later and there are babies everywhere. I sip my Vietnamese iced coffee, wonder about caffeine intake. I don't call him.

6.

Three days later and I'm on a plane, however many miles high we are when we fly. I hold my stomach, think about how it all looks the same as it did when I flew ten years earlier on my way to Disney World after I graduated high school. I hold my stomach, wonder about movement. Wonder if it can tell however high we all actually are. But I'm trying not to think of *it* as it, as anything. And on this plane, flying to a conference cross-country, I hold my stomach, try to eat something, anything. Even if it's just a cracker, there are two weeks of this and I'm trying to be normal.

But it's getting bad and I've been wanting to talk to it. *No, don't think like that.*

Still: I do feel *heavier*, unsure if it is actual or just the weight of knowing.

Scene: Layover, sitting in the Chicago Airport. It won't stop snowing, it should be spring, it should be thawing. There's so much ice, it just won't start thawing. And I can't stop thinking about its features. I keep dreaming about fingernails, about fruit of different sizes.

7.

The size of a peach, that's what the Internet tells me. The size of a peach. So I go to a grocery store, pick one up, hold it in the palm of my hand. It's smaller than I thought it would be. Wasn't I expecting something with more presence, substance? I feel the bruises, the indentations, press my nails into it and make more marks of my own. I put the fuzz up against my face. I wonder about movement.

I walk over to the meat department, pick up a package of raw, red meat. Feel it squish against my fingers, feel my body crave the blood in my mouth. Wonder how the juices would feel dripping down my chin.

I haven't eaten meat in three years, but here I am, deliberating under the bright, white lights of the grocery store. And so I think about iron and irony, think about the life inside of me versus the death in front of me.

Later on, I learn how it has already formed vocal chords. I try not to think about screaming, try not to think how I always want to be screaming.

8.

The person I once loved isn't the person I once loved anymore. Now, he's living above a dive bar, popping pills, working night shifts, back with his ex-girlfriend. He emails me three full days after he finds out what happened, what's happening, one week after I first tried to tell him. He brings over a check that covers half of it. Maybe less than that. I wouldn't take it if I didn't have to take it, and I don't want to feel grateful so I don't feel grateful. He doesn't hug me. We exchange forced pleasantries: He says something about making a life for himself in this town. I tell him how I'm counting the days down until I can get out. He shifts his eyes, not looking directly at me, babbling off a string of excuses about why he can't give me any more money. He leaves my apartment quickly, never even takes his coat off. He smells like cigarettes, like he always does. The scent lingers long after he's gone and it makes my stomach turn.

I think about the people we were when we loved each other. How it felt like there was no rain at all that fall, only sun. And I know it's not true, I know that everything appears bright with light when you're looking back. I know it rained. I know there has to have been rain.

I remember how it didn't seem like our bodies should go together—his so small and wiry, covered in dark hair and acne scars, and mine so much softer, so pale. I wonder how they looked from outside of our bubble.

Here's something I keep coming back to: Despite the direct

physical implications of everything happening, I feel very outside of my body. The thought of him touching me now makes acid rush up to the top of my throat.

Think: The evolution that may be behind protecting myself and what is growing inside of me.

Think: If I saw him under different circumstances, would it feel like it does now?

Think: Am I supposed to feel more than this?

When he comes to my apartment, my clothes are scattered in the living room and since I don't want him in my bedroom, we sit around them. "I'm packing," I tell him. "I need to get out of here for awhile."

He nods, says: "I get that."

9.

I can't eat beforehand, not as if I want to. I can't even drink any orange juice. When my friend and I pull up to the doctor's office, we're the first ones there. Slowly, it seems, the other cars arrive. I fill out paperwork. I say three times: *Yes, this is my first pregnancy.* One room over, as they're taking my blood, I hear a woman explain to the nurse how she already has three children with her husband and they can't have any more right now. She's come alone today. There are pregnant women in the waiting room, and I'm wondering if they can tell just by looking at me.

The medical staff tells me about preventing potential infection, they tell me about the drugs they are putting in my body. They tell me in great detail about the procedure, and they keep calling it that: a procedure. But the nurse makes me feel comfortable, and I spend most of the time waiting for the medicine to kick in. I lay with a heating pad in a white room, shades drawn. The radio is on, it's playing "Only the Good Die Young" and I'm thinking about dramatic irony. I am wondering if I should feel guilt, but once it's started, it is over so quickly. Three vacuum successions and it's over so quickly. I cry four tears out of relief, catch a glimpse of the bright red blood on light blue medical blankets as I'm putting on my pants.

Dazed, dosed, dozing.

It's over so quickly.

The nurse hands me animal crackers and a juice box.

It's over so quickly.

I send him a text message the next morning: *It's over. I'm fine. Don't respond to this. Don't ever contact me.*

It's over.

10.

The doctor tells me:
*because your body has to readjust
you will feel like this for a few months
because your body has to readjust.*

unstable, out of control.

I hear myself saying: *fuck these hormones.*
keep thinking about how my body
is not really my body. Not now,
not these days.

When was the last time my body felt like my own?

There are things they don't tell me—the tenderness of almost everything will continue. I keep wanting to cry at almost everything. Two men touch me in the two weeks that follow and I won't want them to touch me or maybe I will. But I feel so lonely that it's become hard to decide if this specific loneliness can be solved by another person in my bed, by me in someone else's bed. I can't decide if his lips are something I want, and these are the things the doctors don't tell me. The tenderness, the uncertainty of everything will continue.

11.

I go back now and I re-remember things, readjust, write a series of apologies.

I'm sorry i got stoned in that brooklyn loft
i was feeling sick from whiskey or at least
i thought it was from whiskey
i don't know why i didn't know then.
I'm sorry i haven't been feeding you
but both of us won't come out of this
both of us can't come out of this.

i'm sorry i don't feel more sorry.

Sometimes, most times, I feel like I am not grieving properly, and sometimes I feel like I am doing it too loudly. My therapist tells me that I am okay, that it will be okay, that there is no right way to go about any of this, but I can't quite place why I am feeling so sad. It's not like there is a loss of anything. And most times it feels like no one wants to be around me. I feel like nothing is ever going to be the same. This isn't regular grief, this isn't remorse, but it's still some sort of loss.

One week after, the friend who warned of wallowing says: *This has been a dark semester for me,* and all I want to say is: *I'm sorry my abortion has been so hard on you.*

I don't say anything. We keep walking. It's starting to feel like spring outside finally, but rebirth seems like a funny thing to think about and there aren't any leaves on the trees yet, anyway. He stops talking to me soon—most of my friends do.

12.

The doctor tells me: *You are young and healthy. You will be fine by Monday.* But on Monday when I am alone for the first time, I look up pictures of sonograms and ultrasounds and I sob quietly. *You are young and healthy. You will be fine by Monday.* I (re)remember that during the times I was able to sleep after he left me, all I had were pregnancy dreams. I wrote it off as a metaphor, and perhaps it was. What would I have done if I had known the truth then, anyway? So early on, before all those fingernails, those vocal chords, all those tangible fruits of different sizes? Not thirteen or so weeks along like I grew to become, my body getting used to it without me knowing. The length of time when some women decide to start sharing. In the news, a politician refers to pregnant women as vessels, and I want to laugh at the absurdity of it. Think: *Okay, sure, I'm a vessel. I'm a ship. We're in an ocean, there's a leak, I'm sinking slowly.*

13.

I don't want this to mean too much: The morning after, I go to the farmer's market. I grab at plums, compare their size to that of citrus fruits. I press against the hard skin of a grapefruit against the soft skin of my stomach—waiting, wanting to feel something. An ache, an absence. But there's nothing. I don't want this to mean too much: It's March and the market is still being held indoors. It is still too cold outside for flowers to grow anywhere else, but here they are for sale. All these bright blues, purples, pinks. All this grass-green everywhere. And I'm thinking: At least there is spring here. At least life is somewhere.

In my dreams for months after, I am bewildered, but bright. Dizzy and spinning, empty and light. I am walking by new bodies of water, the weather is finally breaking. It's spring. Everywhere must get sunny sometimes.

How to Be

To be a writer

Grow up, slowly and without noticing. Your mom is your best friend. Pick a school close to her. She will ask you to live at home. Shake your head, but cry when she drops you off on your first day. Call her the first night, in tears, and don't hang up until she asks if you'd like for her to come up the next day to have lunch with you. You're practically begging, pleading. Say yes, yes please.

Declare a creative writing major. Your parents are supportive, in contrast, it seems, to everyone else's. Be grateful. Tell your mom your latest story ideas—a girl trapped in a basement, a long-lost sailor returning home to his true love. Send them to her in emails half-finished. In workshop, revise the same stories you've had for years, the ones you wrote in church, and change their titles but not much else. Put together a collection of all the incomplete stories you wrote in high school and give them to your mother for Christmas. She will give you the title suggestion for the would-be book—*I Had a Nickel for a Dream that Costed a Dime*. It will be a long time before you realize that "costed" is not a word.

You are eighteen years old. Write stories about things that you cannot possibly know, or feel. Stories that deal with a pain you have never felt, betrayal you are not familiar with. Sexual experiences you have never had. Think that being a writer means having the craziest ideas. Focus on cool plots and characters that pop, not like people but like pictures, and don't ever wonder what you're really trying to say. Plan out the novels you will write when you are famous.

In workshop all your friends will say, I think I like this but what does it mean? Answer like you think a real writer would, or maybe as if you were a teacher: What do *you* think it means? Think this is what it's like to learn.

It would be helpful at this point to actually write, rather than to just say you'd like to.

If you haven't already, and want *to try something (good lord, anything) else*, go back to page 77.

To fill a heart that still feels empty, go to page 29.

Terra Firma

When Reney's adventures through the pumpjack pulse of the oil fields grew old, she'd climb the fence, wrestle the saddle off the Paint, and place the pad upside down to dry like Pitch had shown her. She might sneak an extra handful of sweetfeed to the colt or let the Blue Heeler Dan George chase her across the tops of round bales, falling down between the bales giggling when the dog came tumbling after her. From the top of the bales, it was easy to see across the Red River to the red, scrubby ridge that was Oklahoma. She watched the stormclouds that skirted them pop and play on the ridge. She waved her hands and shouted in case anybody up there was looking for her, but she never heard anything in return other than a distant roll of thunder.

If she got tired of animal company, she'd pick the hay from her hair and head toward the old farmhouse where Pitch's mama and daddy lived. If the living room was dark except for dust-lightning glittering through the blinds, she'd tip-toe to the back bedroom. There she would crawl into bed beside Nina, click the three-way lamp to the lowest setting, and tap a finger along the row of serial killer biographies and Stephen Kings. Snuggled against Nina's back, she squinted herself into worlds far scarier than any she knew.

Her own bed in the trailerhouse across the drive sometimes stayed made for days. Then her mom, Justine, would come up the steps after work and bang twice before coming in to tell her the crappie were biting or some such and if they hurried they could be back in time to fry fish and potatoes for late supper. Reney never failed to believe in these short evenings—her mom's long black hair absorbing the warm sun, the beer only making her mom happy; Pitch rubbing the small of her mom's back, showing them again and again to let the crappie take all of the minnow before you set the hook; everybody laughing when her mom's hook came up bare. Reney remembered her mom's words before they left Oklahoma. "We'll be a family."

This was something like the family she'd always wanted, the one living out these evenings when the beer brought happy and nobody was talking about steady work or trying to coerce anybody to be somebody they weren't. These evenings, her mom seemed ready to throw out the flattened boxes stored in the racebarn and stay. When the happy spilled over and the voices grew sharp with busted promises and stresses Reney knew too much about, she'd write a note, always giving them an out. *Me and Nina was going to watch a movie. Might fall asleep.* Dan George would meet her on the trailer steps and bite at her legs all the way across the drive.

Pitch's mama was the opposite of Reney's Granny in almost every way. A tiny lady—loud and prone to delightfully creative cursing—she permed her hair at home, snipped the curls herself with her orange-handled sewing scissors. When her slipped disc acted up, she stayed woozy in the back bedroom surrounded by pill bottles and ashtrays, smoking and reading, tugging at the tiny gold pendant that hung around her neck.

Then one morning out of the blue, Reney would wake to find Nina in the kitchen flipping bacon, a cigarette pinched between her lips, ash curling over the skillet. "Garden seed," she'd say, the pitch of her voice registering high amongst the ceiling tiles, "mice been sucking on the end of your hair, girl?"

On these days, Nina attacked the rattletrap farmhouse where Pitch and his daddy were born as if she may never have another chance to set things right. That summer she contact-papered the whole place wood-grained. Wood-grained counters. A wood-grained deep freeze and fridge. She even wood-grained the wooden kitchen chairs and the lid of the toilet seat.

It was on one of these bacon days that Reney followed Nina out the back door and down its sagging steps to the cellar. Reney raised the heavy concrete door enough for an odd rusty weight to counter the door's heft.

"Hey, it's got those teeth just like your necklace," Reney said.

"Drill bit. Chews up earth and spits it out so they can ramrod a pipe into the mud and pull up money," Nina said. "Goddamned useless now." The mare called across the pasture to the stud. "Like most of this Shinola."

She pushed past Reney into the dark cement room. You could hardly find a spot on the floor that wasn't cluttered with hardened race bridles, jangly bits, or boxes of filthy, broken china. Nina opened the vent, lit a cigarette, and twirled a piece of hair around her finger as she surveyed the mess. Reney started by sorting through a box of curled victory pictures but soon stopped on a magazine with a front cover picturing a tremendous cloud of black that spouted three dancing vortices. *Terrible Tuesday* was written in white horror font in the middle of the main cloud.

"What's this?" Reney asked.

Nina reached for the book. "It was a storm. A terrible storm. Fifty people or more died. Wiped out half the town."

"Were you there?"

"Ferrell was. Or I thought he was. Thought it killed him."

Nina flipped the book closed and put it in the trash pile.

"But he was okay?" Reney asked.

"Turned out he'd gone over to Ross Downs to see Pitch ride. Fingers too by-God busted up to call home, but yes, you could say he was okay. Go get us some trash bags."

When they were finished, the cellar looked like the perfect
little jail cell. Coal-oil lamps separated two springy cots covered
with handmade quilts, and they'd maneuvered a bookshelf down the
steps where Nina stored jars of potatoes and green beans put up in a
previous fit of activity. They bought a case of tuna fish and a big tub of
Jif, so much more festive than the black and white commodities from
her Granny's that Reney imagined disasters that would lead her to
unscrew the lid and break the smooth surface with her fingers.

Before she hauled out the trash, Reney snaked *Terrible Tuesday*
out of the bag and hid it between the cot springs and mattress. After
much thought, Reney put *Huck Finn* on the shelf, leaving *It* and the
John Wayne Who-evers for life above ground. She didn't question
their preparations.

Once the cellar was clean, Nina groaned and grasped at pill bottles
when Reney crawled into the bed. Now, she threw an arm over her
eyes if Reney turned on the light. Reney began to experiment with a
limp. She pressed her hand to her hip like Nina when she hobbled to
the bathroom until she was unsure if her pain was imaginary. When
she wasn't on the Paint Horse, she stayed in the cool of the cellar,
leaving the door open, reading, reading, reading. She began to keep her
eye out for driftwood. She squirreled away rope from round bales and
stashed cans of tuna here and there. She saw warnings on the horizon,
kept careful count of the seconds between lightning and thunder.

When the trailer began to strain against the tie-downs or the
shutters of the farmhouse began to bang, Reney was the first and usually
the only one to go to the cellar. She'd light a lamp and spread herself
facedown across a cot, readying her bones for the freight train sound of
a tornado. She whispered pained prayers for her patchwork family who
stayed inside doing dishes, banging on the television, loving, fighting. As
the storm calmed, she never crept up the narrow stairway and leaned her
shoulder into the door until she was certain it had passed.

There wasn't any notice, of course. Pitch, laughing at something her mom said, had hardly stepped onto the farmhouse's front porch to check the clouds when the storm door slammed against the outside wall. The hinges wrenched and moaned terribly against the frame, and Reney swore she felt the house wobble under her feet like the hull of the v-bottom boat did when she stood up too fast. Then, just as quick, the wind reversed course and sucked the door shut. For a moment, Nina, Reney, and her mom stared dumbly at one another, clutching Canasta hands, mouths agape in the glow of Coors Light cans and Nina's special apricot brandy.

It was Nina who reclaimed time, shouting, "My God!" and throwing herself to the door. The metal double-seater rocking chair hung in the splintered limbs of an oak tree. The tire swing had wrapped itself around the naked trunk before coming to a slapping rest, straining against the rope, and blowing back the other way. There was nothing at all on the porch, which before the storm had been cluttered with oil field detritus, muddy boots, horseshoes, and all manner of collected crap dragged in by Pitch and his daddy. Most especially, there was no Pitch. All that was left was a fading roar and the black-orange glow of the evening sky.

Reney's mom hauled her past rattling window panes and out the door. Nina bowed in the wind on the last step, shouting Pitch's name. Reney grasped her cuff as they bounded past. Heavy drops of rain pelted them, sparsely at first. By the time they reached the cellar door, the rain beat their bodies so violently that Reney could not hear what her mom was shouting, could barely see her mouth O-ing words into the storm. Reney strained toward the sky looking for some sign of Pitch's boots, hoping to catch the flash of his grin or the sound of his voice as he passed over, imagining him huddled over, going to the bat, riding the cloud to victory.

Before she knew it, she was clinging to her mother, crashing into the hole. Their wet bodies mashed together, pulling and grunting into the cramped, cool stairwell. It took both of them to hold onto the concrete door so Nina could latch it. Reney could hear Nina sobbing once the storm was muffled, could hear her fumble open the cellophane of a new pack of Merits.

A lighter clicked. Nina's face glowed, then darkened.

"Give me one," Reney's mom said. The thin, yellow light led them down the steps. The lighter clicked again, and Reney's mom was briefly illuminated.

Reney felt for the lamp, her fingers lifting the glass bulb and rolling the wick by habit. When the light settled on the room, there was Pitch huddled in the far corner. He held his knees tight to his chest, and when he saw them, he took a deep breath and spat between his legs.

"The wind," he said. "It took a pumpjack weight right off the porch. Spiraled up like a piece of paper."

There was a moment when everything, to Reney, seemed like it was going to be fine. And some seconds that her mom, too, must have felt relief. Nina rushed to Pitch and took his head to her tiny hip and rocked him there, saying "My boy, my baby, my baby boy" over and over like that.

"We thought you were gone," Reney's mom said. "Thought the wind took you." An accusation. She tapped the cigarette with her index finger three times and reached to open the vent. The night flashed through the slats. Reney waited for thunder.

"Thought I was goddamn going to die," Pitch said.

"Did you think about anybody but yourself?"

Nina put a hand on the small of her back and shuffled over to a cot and laid down. She twirled a curl and hung her cigarette hand off the cot. Reney's mom didn't say anything else, which to Reney was the weirdest thing she could have done. Instead she clicked on the radio and started spinning the knob across the static. Pitch dusted off his backside, and Reney thought he might say sorry.

Outside, the sky still popped and shook the window with thunder bumpers, as Pitch called them, but the roar of the wind was already letting up. Reney still hadn't heard the freight train. She took her opening.

"Did you see it, Pitch?"

"Just that weight. It was more the sound and the force of the thing."

"If you'd a had your lariat, you could have roped it."

Pitch poked her in the ribs. "Maybe held it until you got there to tickle the damn thing into submission."

"You think Dan George is okay? The horses?"

"Animals have their ways."

"Two kids," Reney's mom said, her eyes still on the radio that wasn't picking anything up.

Pitch cut his eyes.

"I said I didn't know I was getting two kids out of this deal. But I should have."

Reney's heart lurched. She slumped over to the end of Nina's cot. Before she could sit down, Pitch kicked the bookshelf, knocking a low shelf loose. Cans of tuna scattered across the floor and the Jif jar busted. His quick violence still surprised Reney. She'd only seen it on occasions when her mom wouldn't stop nagging, and once when the stud kicked him bad in the thigh. Pitch looked at the mess in the floor and shook his head, like he was trying to decipher something just beyond reach.

"You made it clear my pockets ain't big enough." His face didn't look like Pitch anymore. "Now I ain't man enough to fight off a tornado, so I imagine you ought to start taping together boxes like you've been threatening to do since you got here. If you want to get back across that Red River, I ain't stopping you."

Reney wondered what her Granny was doing. She thought of the soft one-dollar bills her Granny had sent for her birthday, the sweet chicken scratch letters. She remembered the last time she'd talked to her on the phone and how she'd told her Granny she had to go because she wanted to help Pitch wash the stud, how she'd cried that night in bed feeling bad about it. Each night since, she would dream her Granny's brown skin into being, feel the curve of her arthritic fingers in her own. They'd take their cane poles to the Lawson's pond and catch perch for supper, and her Granny would wipe cornmeal on her big, aproned belly. Then together they'd sing the sun up. Always too early, Reney would wake in North Texas. Even as she wiped her Granny from her eyes, the sound of the stud blowing snot and stamping outside her window always made Reney smile.

The wind grabbed the heavy door from Pitch and slammed it against the ground before he could wrestle it shut. Maybe for good, Reney thought. She started after him, but her mom caught her. She pulled Reney's face into her chest. Reney tried not to cry, tried to banish the pictures of twirling vortices carrying Pitch away. Her mom whispered, *Sorry.*

"He promised me," her mom said. "When I quit my job to come down here, he promised me. Hell, Nina, we aren't hardly bringing in enough to keep the place you gave us lit. There's a rig going up over by Sunset, but I can't get him over there to apply. He's not lazy. What's wrong with him?"

"He's just like his daddy," Nina said. "Don't want to be tied down." She tapped another cigarette out, lit it, and sat up. She was so tiny her toes only brushed the concrete floor. Ferrell wasn't hardly ever around. Tonight he was on a trip to Kansas looking at a mare nobody could afford. He was big fun when he was there, always trying to get her to do the circle game and making Reney look, then giving her a playful thump on her arm when she did. Nina cackled at his foolery when people were around. Other times, she mostly shook her head, if she responded at all.

"Ain't never going to change," Nina said. "He'll love you, but he'll be looking for a runner or running that river until the day he dies. There's a lot to love about them. More to hate, so I'll tell you like I told the last one. If you can't take it, you better leave now."

Reney's mom kissed her head and sniffed. Reney considered her life back home: her Granny, growing older, Reney knew, by the day. Her mom's double shifts. The second job at the track bar. The first husband, then the shared houses. The parade of boyfriends with big buckles and talk who promised microscopes and telescopes and puppies and all manner of things a stringy-haired mixed-blood girl might dream of. Pitch had a mad streak for sure. You had to work hard to find it, though. Reney figured the walls or bookshelves could take it. She'd seen worse.

"Leave if you want," Reney said. "I'm staying." Then she ran up the stairs and into the storm.

The rain was just an idea now. Overhead, she could hear big boughs sway and settle, hear the tiny limbs click. The thunder didn't feel like it was exploding from her skull outwards. She pulled her T-shirt over her head and ran to the driveway where she watched Pitch's taillights bounce over the cattleguard and float into the sky.

She jumped when her mom took her hand and kissed her palm. Her mom held tight, though, laced their fingers.

"I'm so sorry, honey."

The taillights disappeared at the highway turn. They watched the white glow of headlights push through the night on an even plane toward town. Dan George came trotting up, shivering and soaked.

"We was going to be a family." Reney pulled her hand away so Dan George could lick it.

"Me and Pitch just got some things to work out. You deserve better."

"You don't understand him at all. I wish you'd quit making him run off."

"Reney, life don't run on trinkets and giggles. I've worked two jobs since I was sixteen to make sure you wasn't raggedy. I wanted us to stay in Oklahoma. I had a good job. You was in school. We had Lula and Granny." Her voice trailed as she looked over at the trailer house. The porch light was flickering with a short she'd been after Pitch to fix. "He couldn't bear to part with the Red River."

"Everything wasn't great there either, so don't act like it was," Reney said. She kissed Dan George and was halfway up the trailerhouse steps and through the door before she heard her mom call her name.

Reney spread a towel on her quilt and patted for Dan George to join her. She wrapped herself around him and rested her forehead on his. The bookshelf was bothering Reney. It made her think of the swollen mess the first husband had made of her mom's face. She remembered the terrible weeping, how her mom had hardened when Reney walked in, then smiled and said it would all be okay. She'd hastily put on too much makeup, then put all of his clothes in the hallway of their apartment building and changed the locks for good. Reney had wanted to let him in when he came weeping at the door, though she couldn't remember, now, why.

Reney heard the door close. When her mom sat on the edge of the bed, Reney squeezed her eyes shut. She wanted to sit up and let her mom hug her and tell her how she was the most important thing in the world in her way of looking deep into Reney so that Reney knew it was true no matter what had happened to the contrary. As her mom smoothed her hair, Reney's heart began to fill with love in the way it had of feeling like it might burst. She wanted to sit up and say, *You are my family, Mama. No matter where we are, you are my family.* But then she thought of Pitch and the tornado and how he must have been scared. And how maybe her mom didn't know the first thing about being scared because all she knew was love and mad and love and mad all over again. So Reney kicked her leg, feigned sleep, and rolled toward the wall.

Her mom shooed the dog. She outlined Reney's bent legs with her own, pulled Reney into her, and clasped the top of Reney's hand. Reney could hear from her mom's breathing that she was crying. They lay like that, Reney thinking to herself, I'm going to turn over now, *I'm going to turn over now and say sorry, I'm going to turn over now* until her mom sniffed one last time in the way her mom could have of turning off sad, like it was a radio and you could just stop the sounds and all the feelings would go away.

"I know you can hear me, and I know you love me," her mom said. "It's okay that you aren't going to talk right now. Mama's got to go to town, baby. I'll make it all right. You wake up scared, you go get Nina. You can go on over there now if you want. Mama and Pitch will both be back soon. We'll be okay. Don't let that dog back up here. He has fleas, and he stinks."

Her mom got up and moved to the door. Reney could feel her, knew she didn't leave.

"I know you love Pitch, Reney. I guess I love Pitch, too. He's just Pitch, is all. But I love you more than anything in the whole wide world."

They couldn't know it, but the storm had only meandered that night. Even as her Mom's truck roared to life, powered by the grace of dead dinosaurs and desperate love, the system was wrapping back around itself where it would settle on top of the old farmhouse and trailer. There it would stay, intent on letting out all of its howling fight on the five-acre stickerpatch sucked dry of oil, useless for growing anything but the horses a certain breed of man's dreams. Heartbreakers. All Reney knew as she lay there listening to her Mom's truck rattle over the cattleguard was that, outside, the horses were sleeping upright and anywhere they could be heard, her mom's words were true.

How to Be

A void

Sit in a coffee shop alone, where no one knows your name, and write. Sit in the corner of a bookstore alone, where people look at you strangely, and write. Sit in a library alone, where no one talks to each other, and write. Become a Starbucks regular. Rotate between the three in your town. Haunt independently owned coffee shops. Don't bother to learn the names of the employees. Lurk in corner booths, in window seats. Gravitate to the two outlets. Eat your meals there, if you eat at all. And write.

Realize that you were always going to end up here, no matter what you chose.

Think to yourself there is beauty in heartbreak and pretty words in pain, but remember that everyone uses the point of a pen to stitch up a broken heart. Stop acting like you have something to offer to the world (and to him) that is somehow different than what other people have.

Write new stories. Ones with hearts that beat, that breathe, that bleed. Understand finally that fiction is not made up at all. Wonder if it is possible to be a good writer and also to be happy. Think immediately that this is a stupid question. Realize that wasn't an answer. Recognize that you would trade these words in an instant for a taste of something like happiness, but see also that you never had a choice. Understand that the pain was necessary in order for your writing to grow, and the writing was necessary in order to stand the heartbreak—the chicken, the egg, what came first, the writing or the pain?

At this point, stop showing your mother what you're working on.

Dementia, 1692

We heard my mother scream just before daylight. The house was bathed in a blue pre-sunlight and the color was the very sound of her wails. She had been trying to sit up with my younger sister but had fallen asleep and when she woke my sister was cold, her mouth open just a little, even the red of the rash gone white.

It was a year before that she and I had cracked open an egg on the scalloped side of a hand mirror. I cupped its two halves in my hands, pouring the yolk from one half shell to the other so that the white dripped heavily onto the glass. She held the pewter handle of the mirror and swirled the egg like batter on a griddle, the way Tatuba had taught us to do if we wanted to see our future.

Who will love us? We whispered to the glass and I crossed my fingers behind my back that in the eggy mirror would appear the face of John Tucker, the blacksmith's son. We waited, watching, heads together, and I could feel my sister's breath on my arm. I saw our twisted mouths in the mirror and I giggled but just then, Beth gasped and dropped the mirror, letting it fall where it landed face down but did not crack.

Skull! She palmed her cheeks. I saw a skull!

I rolled my eyes and picked up the mirror and wiped the soapy egg off with the frayed corner of my apron. The three-legged cat was already licking the floor clean.

Really! I did, I did! She grabbed onto my arm and I could see she really was afraid.

Ssshhh, I whispered, without tenderness, for it was too late, the tall Indian stood in the doorway. Tatuba looked at the mirror and the eggshell on the table, one half spilling yellow, and clicked her tongue. My sister ran to her and told her what she'd seen, crying now, saying that she would surely die. Tatuba held her to her skirts and said softly, Nah, some witch fooling you. But before taking her into the kitchen for some milk, she turned to me and scowled.

I stood alone and looked at the streaked mirror, its aging glass speckled black. I squinted hard but could only see my own pale face with its hook nose. My eyes the exact color of the mud that I had that morning scraped from my boot tread with a stick.

It started with a pink eye and a fever. Tatuba gave her root broth and sent her to bed. The next day she was no better and the third day she had the rash. The whole of her body was spotted red, like a pig's belly. My mother cried out when Tatuba asked her to come look and the doctor was sent for.

Dr. Phipps confirmed that it was measles and told us to wash her eyes and mouth with boiled water twice a day. I stayed in Tatuba's room. One night as she put me to sleep in her bed, I asked her when Beth would get better. She stared at me for a moment and then took my sister's hairbrush from her apron pocket and pulled a nest of yellow hair from it. Using a strand of her own long black hair, she tied the nest into a small faceless doll, with only a head and a limbless body. Then she knelt and reached beneath her bed, pulling out a small wooden box. She took out a stub of a black candle and lit it on the lamp already burning on her small table. As she tilted the candle sideways, the black wax dripped slowly onto the doll, right where the heart would be. She chanted words from Barbados, the same words, over and over again like a song, quiet and fast.

When she was done, Tatuba blew out both candles and put the doll under the pillow we shared. I watched the wicks still smoking in the moon-filled room and wondered if a witch was watching us at that very moment. I snuggled closer to Tatuba's warm body but kept an eye open for signs in the darkness, waiting with both fear and desire.

A few months before my sister died, I did an evil thing. It was the neighbor's black and white dog, a mean and mangy mutt. One day, as I was waiting on the neighbor's porch for my mother to finish her visit, I told the dog, who was lying on the step, to get out of the way. Git, I said, and pointed, but the dog only looked at me and bared his broken teeth. So I gently nudged his flank with the toe of my boot, and he turned and bit me on the shin. It didn't break the skin, but tore my dress and left four teardrop bruises where his teeth had been.

I cried and my mother came out and scolded me. Don't you know anything? she said. Let sleeping dogs lie?

I wished that night with all my might, my hands squeezing together, that the dog would die.

Two weeks later, it was dead. Just like that. I thought it, and it happened.

I hadn't wished my sister dead, but I watched Tatuba make that doll and that dull black wax fell on her disembodied hair and I thought, *that won't help*, and the next day she was gone. Besides, we looked into the future and had seen the skull. We invited the death she saw then into our lives. The guilt of these memories was all I could think of, until even my grief became a shadow to it. I stayed awake at night, wondering if death would come for me, too. I broke the mirror with a rock, cracking it quick and quiet. I said it was an accident. And that I had accidentally cut myself, even though it was really a sweet and welcome relief when I pried out a wedge of broken glass, cutting my fingers, the drops of blood falling to the fragments of my image in what I hoped would be both redemption and inoculation.

Years later I still think of that dog, and know it was not me that killed it, of course it wasn't, but still I am unable to divorce the memory of my throbbing bone with a raw and hungry guilt. It is as if my sister's death lives in that spot on my shin, and I can finger that smooth skin and feel over and over again that I did something wrong. That it should have been me.

Eventually I told my mother about the mirror and the doll and begged her not to tell Tatuba I had told her. I told her about the dog, too. She told me it was not my fault, any of it, and stroked my hair until I slept a child's sleep again. Still I longed to ask Tatuba if one always knew one was a witch, or if it could sneak up inside you, like a bad habit.

But there was no more talk of magic, white or black, until two years after my sister's death, when the neighbor's children became ill. The sickness started with seizures: strange jerky movements that seemed to rust their joints even while they were standing. They spoke nonsense. The youngest had been heard barking like a dog, even, and had red marks the size of a child's bite into an apple all over her little body.

The neighbor, Jane Good, was beside herself and came to my mother crying one afternoon. Tatuba was sweeping the kitchen and I was sitting in the corner sewing my first quilt. Mother sent me out to gather chicory, a fool's errand, but as I left I heard Mother Good say that her children were undoubtedly bewitched, and that her husband said he knew who had done it all right.

Widow Smithson lived on the edge of town in a house half fallen-down, with one side collapsed and broken so you could see clear through from front to back. The other side had a tight little room just barely listing away from the collapsed side. She piled kindling, dead and crooked branches, everywhere in her yard. She fed all sorts of animals, so dogs, cats, and birds hung around the yard, too. She had no teeth and stringy gray hair and people said she drank. She traded with Indians, and sometimes had a bright red stone around her neck. There were hundreds of glass jars in her half-felled house, jars filled with the leaves of dried plants and animal hair and horns. For a fee, she would vanish your warts or heal your pox. She could also tell the future by reading your own hand like a book. Though now, most people went to Dr. Phipps, especially after the new reverend called her work white magic and deemed it "of the Devil."

I found a few stalks of chicory and, gathering the corn blue flowers in my apron pocket, I headed back to the yard where I could see tall Tatuba, shaking out Pa's wet pants to hang. I watched her stern face as she clipped flapping legs to the line.

Come help me, child, she said when she saw me. She handed me a damp blue dress of my own to hang and as I did she looked toward the kitchen door and then reached into her apron pocket and pulled out a small white nugget on a piece of twine. This, she told me, is a black rabbit's tooth. It's for protection. I want you to wear it under your dress, and then put it under your pillow at night. If that spirit's got them Good children, it might get hungry for you, too.

I put the tooth to my nose. It smelled like nothing, like snow. Tatuba tied it around my neck and I tucked the long nub under my dress just before Mother called to me.

The Good children became the talk of Salem. The following Sunday during sermon, Reverend Mathers asked us to pray for them. The three, all towheaded, were sitting in the front row. As he called on the Lord to help battle the Devil that besieged them, the youngest Good girl, the one that had the bite marks, a curly-haired cherub of a child, began howling out like a kicked dog. The whole congregation shifted and whispered, like restless water. Mother herself went flourwhite and grasped me to her hard. Still the child bayed. Reverend Mathers preached above the howls, yelling at us to pray that the Devil would let this child be. He grew more and more angry as he yelled at us and at the Devil. His tall thin body paced and preached and paced quicker and quicker, his spindly hands flying about him, and even from where I sat I could see the spit spraying from his mouth. As he smacked fist to palm again and again, I felt the little rabbit's tooth against my sternum, and rolled it across the bone under my dress. My mother and several other women were crying when Reverend Mathers finally stopped his sermon, took a bowl of holy water, and dumped it over the child's head.

The room went silent. The child was still and Reverend Mathers leaned over and stroked her wet hair. She seemed to see, then, that all gathered were looking at her, and she started to cry. The congregation sat in still and silent awe.

They arrested Widow Smithson the next day.

I still remember the unearthly wails of that child. A meeting house, quiet and orderly, completely swallowed by that high and even sound. Indeed, as time passed, and all that was to happen happened, it seemed that all of us disappeared into the small black gaping hole in that child's angel face. We were not impervious. A girl's mouth. All it took. I think that and I feel that old fear. That old desire. Smoking wicks in the moony dark.

A few days later Mrs. Good came over in her work dress. I was in the yard trying to get the three-legged cat out from under a cart when she came. Child, she said, hurrying to me. Then she looked around before she reached into her apron and pulled out a jar of yellow water.

Child, give this to Tatuba, or your Mother, and for the heaven's sake, do not open it and do not let anyone see. Not your pa, you hear?

I nodded and took the jar as she turned and walked quickly

away. I watched her body rock, her large bottom toddling away as she disappeared down the road. Then I walked slowly to the kitchen door, examining the contents of the jar on the way, tipping it up and down to catch the sunlight.

I put it on the table with a smack so that Tatuba would look up from her darning. It's from Mrs. Good, I said.

Good Lord, child, get that off the table. Here, give it to me.

I grabbed it and held it back for a minute. What is it? I started to open the jar. Is it tinkle? I asked. It looks like tinkle. Tatuba grabbed for the jar, but I was quicker. I put my hand on the lid, and started to twist it. I had to hold it carefully to keep any of the liquid from sloshing out while I grinned my threat at Tatuba's scowling face.

Tatuba signed and said, Child, that's for a *witch* cake, so don't you play.

I immediately put the jar in her hand. She knew she'd won with that one word, witch, and picked up the jar, turning away, taller.

I followed her and pulled her skirt a little. Tell me, I said, tell me.

She sighed and looked out the open kitchen door. When she spoke, it was a whisper. One can see if someone is bewitching another by making a witch cake. You make it from rye meal and the piss of one bewitched. This, she said, wrapping the jar in a cloth, is of the littlest Good girl.

But how do we know from the cake? I asked, too loud.

We don't know, sshh. Tatuba put the jar in the bottom of an empty wash basin. We know when we feed the cake to a dog. You see a witch's invisible spirit, some of her venomous wisps, go into the body of the one she bewitches, and is even in that there, she said, pointing to the covered jar. Once we feed that cake to the dog, the witch will feel herself being chewed by a dog. The witch will scream in pain at the same time the dog is eating the cake.

So how will we know if Widow Smithson is screaming? She's in jail.

Your mother and Mrs. Good will feed the cake to one of the Good's dogs and at the same time I will go visit her in jail.

So you think she is the real witch?

I don't know, she said quietly. I don't think so, but that's why we make the cake. So we know.

Decades later, my mother's own widowed mind would flee. One of her last completely lucid nights, she would tell me that she had always blamed Tatuba for my sister's death. Not because of the mirror or the doll but because, did I not remember, Tatuba had been traveling the week before, to market in Boston to buy cloth for the Salem ladies. It was undoubtedly her that had brought the measles into the house. She would tell me, as firelight flickered against her open hands, that she had decided that it was God's will, then, that she condemn Tatuba.

The day the cake was baking the house smelled like the woods in the summer heat when all the plants start to sweat their scents all over. They barely let it cool before they took the cake tin outside and set it on the back stoop next to a mangy gray dog that Mrs. Good had brought over. Tatuba had already gone into town and was, at high sun, supposed to be at the jail. I watched from the kitchen window as the dog ate the cake happily, pulling her lip up to show yellow teeth as she picked it apart. She licked the last crumbs and Mother and Mrs. Good looked satisfied, and they brought the tin inside and sat down and waited.

It turned out Widow Smithson did not cry out or scream in the jail and Tatuba was triumphant when she returned home. I said it, didn't I, child? She patted my cheek, I said no way is that harmless old lady a witch.

Mother suggested they write Reverend Mathers an anonymous note saying that he had perhaps arrested the wrong woman. But

Tatuba thought telling him right out would be better. They spent the rest of the afternoon talking softly about who the real witch might be, Tatuba mending socks, Mother drinking tea.

Tatuba didn't come home the next day after market and Mother sat up all night, long after the last candle had burned to its nub. The next morning Pa took her to town to inquire, which is when Reverend Mathers somehow convinced Mother that Tatuba's cake was nothing more than a ruse, played on herself and Mrs. Good, in an attempt to free Widow Smithson, her sister in Devil-worship.

She would, he told her, be asked to testify at Tatuba's trial.

As her mind went, Mother's hair went from glossy black to stone gray within two months. She was no longer a woman, but a *sick* woman or, to the village children, a *crazy* woman, not unlike—I thought one morning as I walked her through town and saw two small girls pointing at her and whispering—not unlike Widow Smithson had seemed to me as a child.

When she still had some faculties, Mother told me she was cursed, that the witches had come for their revenge. When she lost her way home, she would tell the neighbors that a witch had put a spell on her path, moving familiar oaks and posts, to lead her astray. She would shake her head and cluck then, looking up to the cloudless sky in resignation to the Lord, or perhaps it was to Tatuba.

It seemed to comfort her, her imagined persecution, and was her one point of clarity for which I was grateful, though I had never believed Tatuba a witch. Others, maybe, but not her, with her soft brown hands that were always gentle in my hair, and her pretty voice singing songs from church. But it didn't bother me to think of my mother's illness as Tatuba's revenge. It made me, in fact, a woman of thirty, feel like I was a child again, listening carefully for Tatuba's footfall. Ready to tell her spirit that I understood, and would not betray her again. Ready, too, to ask her for mercy on my mother's behalf.

Summer swelled as the day of the trial came. Mother didn't want to go but Pa told her she would. He said if she did not, she would likely hang, too.

I wasn't allowed to go, as children were not permitted, except in this case the Good children, and I was left to watch them disappear down the road in Pa's cart. As I waited for them to return, I went into the yard to the edge of the woods and untied the rabbit's tooth from my neck. I took a stick and scraped a hole in the hard black dirt underneath a sycamore tree. I laid the rabbit's tooth in its shallow grave and whispered over it to protect Tatuba now. And Mother, I added, before folding the earth back over it.

When they came home, Mother went straight to bed, so I had to wait for the next day to hear that she had told the court about the mirror, the doll, my sister's death. I screamed at her that she was a traitor and stomped outside, where I fell asleep crying under the sycamore tree, my body cradled over the buried tooth.

When I awoke I was empty, feeling as if my heart, too, had seeped underground. I had betrayed Tatuba once by telling Mother about the mirror and the doll, and now I had betrayed her again when Mother told the whole of the world.

Mother began to cackle and start at the very children that pointed at her. She did this, she said, because she was a witch. Did I not know? She started to drool, and refuse her bath. Her hair become gnarled, her face sunken. Dr. Phipps, an old man himself, gave me a sedative for the nights when she would rage and scream from the porch. Asking the sky to come and get her already.

I only saw Tatuba once more, the day she was hung in the square. She looked taller and fiercer than ever on the scaffolding. The whole town was gathered. I watched her eyes, so white against her skin, and I both hoped she wouldn't look at me and hoped she would. Finally she did and gave me a sad smile. I thought I heard her say, *Child*, just as they kicked the stool she stood on, and there was a knock and a snap and then just the creak of the gallows' frame as she swung there. I saw her eyes stop seeing even though they were open and I felt like this was the skull my sister saw in the eggy mirror. Tatuba's. Her feet swung and I wanted to go to her, to hold her skirts and still them. I wanted her to shoo me off of her one more time, but Mother dragged me away.

Mother grew worse, unable in the end to even feed herself, before she finally died. One morning I went to wake her, and she was cold, half of her face had gone slack in a way that reminded me of Widow Smithson's half-fallen house. I buried her next to my sister and Pa in the Salem cemetery and as I began to grow old myself, my own dark hair streaking with gray, I wondered if my mind would go, too.

Widow Smithson died in jail a few months after Tatuba's death, but nobody seemed to notice as Reverend Mathers had revealed that the Devil had indeed besieged us and witches were everywhere. I never went to another hanging, though there were several as I grew taller. I didn't live in fear of being bewitched, only the lingering fear that I was a witch and that Tatuba had somehow known this, which is why she had taught me some of her white magic, why she had looked at me with that sad smile as they kicked the stool out from under her bare feet. My suspicions were only made worse when Reverend Mathers published his pamphlet on the identification of witches. Among the numerous symptoms was a preternatural teat on the body, which is not sensitive to the touch. I had a mark just like that below my right hip, one that I could not feel, no matter how much I fingered it in my bed in the night. It made me sure I was not innocent, even as I knew I couldn't harm anyone—that I was untrained and impotent, protected still by Tatuba and the rabbit's tooth I had unburied after her death. I clung to its white dullness in the dark, feeling that old fear, that old shame, but no longer any desire, nor any curiosity to know magic.

In the end, it was my eyesight that failed me. Now, I fumble around the furniture, alone in my darkness, and hear the world outside edging around me. I feel them seeing me, a lonely old woman. Children throw stones at the house, the cracking sounds sharp and startling. After they are gone, I go out and feel for the stones around the side of the foundation and when I find them I bring them in and put them on my shelf. I roll them in my palms from time to time and try to guess their color. The youngest Good child, now an old woman herself, brings me a basket of food each week. She leaves it on the porch and does not knock and I let her think I can't hear her steps coming and going softly, though I would like to ask her about those days when she howled in the meeting house. I think of almost nothing but that time: of my sister's freckled face, of the mirror, the jar of yellow, Tatuba's hands, the dog eating the cake with greedy and indifferent judgment, and I think of the Widow, dying alone in the gloom of the jail, and Mother, relieved even as her mind slipped away, and me, here in the dark, waiting. Waiting for Tatuba to come and pull my dress up, point at my unfeeling mark, my witch's teat, and shout to whomever will listen that I am not who I seem, and never have been, and I think this waiting, this, too, is punishment.

How to Be

Call home

Remember that your family will always let you come back. You will forever, no matter what, have a place to call home in your mother's arms. But it will not feel like home anymore. Hug your mother when you return but thrash against the embrace. Breathe her in and choke on the smell. Try to remember that you missed her, even though it's hard to believe that now.

You are twenty-three years old. Move back into your childhood room, a time capsule from your senior year of high school. Stare at pictures of a much younger you next to a mother that looks just like yours but knows everything about her daughter. Take down the pictures of your old friends. Sleep every night with your dog. Start looking for a job in the suburbs, the local Half Price Books, maybe. Make minimum wage. Your parents will not make you pay rent. Do not consider moving out again for a long, long time. Get drinks on Saturday night with your one friend left from high school. She has plans to move to California.

Fight with your mother. About politics. About religion. About existing. When you are not fighting with her, ignore her. Lie to her about where you're going, where you've been, what you had to drink. She still thinks the only things you eat are pizza bagels and fruit snacks. She has never tasted Indian food at your favorite restaurant or seen you eat broccoli. Smoke in the car and change your clothes before you go in. Leave the cigarettes in the console and lock the door. Start a new novel but don't have a plot, just a really angry protagonist. Throw away the classified ads your mother brings home for you.

Wonder if it is possible that the golden-eyed boy would agree to try again if you called. Think even a life in an office away from your family would be better than this, a life on hold. Remember the way he had one tuft of black hair that always stood straight up. Remember that you could jump on his back with no warning and he would always catch you piggy-back style. Remember that he had 188 freckles on his body. Remember that your mother loved him.

Hesitate with your hand on the phone, your thumb on the first digit of his number. Take a deep breath. Call. Say hello in your most you're-not-really-average voice. Grab your notebook, your pen, your laptop, your words, and go to page 55 when he hangs up.

Better Than Six

10:00 a.m. The sky is ominous. Bruised. Like a scraped-up leg. (Like that time she flew off the bike and he came running.) A hidden sun stains the low-lying clouds: green, black, blue, gray, reddish-yellow in places. The sky looks grotesque. ("Your leg might need stitches," the doctor said.) She's got to stop for gas. The fuel gauge is nearing empty. The gas station's a block away. Might as well be a mile. Both directions, bumper-to-bumper. (At the sight of it, she'd cried. For the beat up leg as much as the pain.) The road here in downtown is red brick, not asphalt. Orange, white, and purple flowers wilt in planters that've been placed at intervals along the sidewalk. The shopping center to her right currently caters to people with high end tastes in pet food, antiques, and garden gnomes. The businesses there rotate in and out. Twenty years back, she remembers, it housed a record store, a travel agency, and a dry cleaners. All that's left is the Corner Diner Café. Its one-story façade is more or less unchanged. The cracked shutters are blue. There are flowers on the sill. The Corner Diner Café has outlasted economic up- and downturns, not to mention the recent trend in gentrifi-beautification. It's been fifteen years since she was here last.

10:05. Beneath the bruised sky, everything appears deserted. Somewhere up ahead, just a mile or two away, a funeral is about to happen. Right now, it's hard to believe anything can happen. At the moment, on the storm's edge, everything appears suspended: the lights brighter, the outlines starker. This whole traffic-jammed-up world: weightier. The gas station's green-and-white sign—Guzzle n' Go!—glows eerily against the blue-black clouds. Guzzle n' Go, she thinks. An ironic name. Traffic is at a standstill. All guzzle, no go. A pre-storm pause. Right before all hell breaks loose. If traffic doesn't move, she might miss the funeral, which starts in twenty-three minutes.

10:07. She glances at the sky and allows it to remind her of the time she flew off the bike and he came running. Her eyes shift from the dramatic sky to the folded up newspaper in the passenger's seat. His obituary. It arrived several days ago. She was surprised to find her name listed among his survivors. Amon Grant, dearly departed, is survived by his loving wife Heidi and his three children, Brandon, Ashley, and Grace. There's quite a bit of history that sentence decks over. Quite a bit of turbulent water beneath the rickety bridge and Grace. In fact, she's not quite sure the conjunctive structure will hold much longer. Long enough for a funeral? Perhaps.

10:12. The world seems suspended. The only thing moving is the traffic light up ahead. Despite the standstill, it dutifully rotates through its signals: golight, green; slowlight, yellow; stoplight, red. Neither lane has moved in twelve minutes.

10:15. She's still stuck. The first drops of rain are falling. She can't get it out of her head now: that time she flew off her bike and he came running. Ever since she got the call—Grace, it's Heidi, your step-mom. I know we've never met. I'm so sorry, your father wanted to reach out to you, he just didn't know how. Now it's too late. I'm so sorry to tell you your father's passed on—scraps of memory have fluttered to the surface. Like the news of his death caused a wind to sweep through the void his absence left, stirring up twenty-year-old debris, driving the detritus of memory with it. Trying to seize those pieces is like trying to catch wind-tossed paper scraps. Is there enough there to reconstruct a whole man? Probably not. She was six years old when he left. She hasn't seen him since.

10:21. Yes, that's all she has of him—scraps. Nonetheless, his death is an imperative. It forces her to go back and try to piece him together. Sitting in her stalled car, looking at the storm's bruised beginnings, she can't help but remember her scraped-up leg from the time she flew off her bike. And he came running. Raindrops splotch up the windshield now, making red round sparkles of brake lights. The sky is darker than before. She supposes she should look for a weather report. Her hand on the steering wheel stays put. Amon Grant…dearly departed… survived by. Read right, that statement is accurate enough. Amon Grant departed her life twenty years ago. The price for his absence was dear. Most importantly, she survived him.

10:23. The rain is picking up. So is the wind. It jostles the car. People are abandoning their vehicles and heading for the only two things open: the diner and the gas station. The ones without umbrellas run hunched over. She stays put. The banged up sky entrances her. All those colors—green, yellow, black, blue, red. It's surreal. Like the memory of her leg twenty years ago. What a stupid thought. She can't get it out of her head. She stared at her calf as it discolored with blood below the skin (bruise) and blood upon the skin (deep cut)…

10:24. Spellbound, she watches drops of rain rhythmically explode the green golight across her windshield—splat—wiper time: again, and again and again and… The wipers can't keep up. The rain's a torrent. She shuts them off. Across her windshield: a green mess of yellow mess of red mess of light… Thunder peals overhead. Wind violently shakes the car. Seen through the rain, the gas station's green-and-white Guzzle n' Go sign seems to drizzle down her windows endlessly.

A wicked-witch style (her mother's style) meltdown. More people are emerging from of their cars. She imagines the crowds gathering inside the diner and the gas station. Bumper-to-bumper without, elbow-to-elbow within. Wait. Suddenly, it occurs to her—a tornado might be coming. If so, the car is the last place she should be. She considers getting out. She stays put.

10:25. A scrap of memory, just within reach—Her leg! It needed five stitches! How could she have forgotten? She was petrified. She'd never been to the hospital, never needed one stitch, much less five. Her father had taken her hand and said, "Better than six." Then he'd smiled, so she'd smiled. He'd laughed, so she'd laughed. And shortly thereafter, just two days later, he'd left. Those two days were the pre-storm pause, right before hell (which, yes, hath no fury like her mother's) broke loose.

10:27. The traffic light quits mid-rotation. The Guzzle n' Go sign dims. Must be a blackout. A power outage. The world darkens. It drowns. Five minutes to go. Better than six! Is that where that stupid phrase comes from? Ever since she can remember, she's said "better than six" to mean "could've been worse." She'd never considered its origins. It had always just been a reflexive phrase, like the bless you that follows up a sneeze, but…is it possible?

10:30. The funeral is now. "He would've wanted you there," Heidi had tearfully said in her call. "He wanted to reach out…So proud of you for going to med school…" Guess the bastard kept tabs. The wind howls, the rain pours, the thunder drowns. The sky's a mess. The car's in shadow. The lights on the dashboard are eerily bright. All she can see are outlines. All she can think are scraps. His hand on hers. His eyes. Green flecked with brown. Reflexively, she glances in the rearview mirror. She can't see a thing. Hail strikes the roof, the windshield. Ping, ping—crack! Fuck! Suddenly, she's screaming. It's ridiculous, why, why is she screaming. The lightning begins in earnest. Bolts illuminate her eyes locked on the rearview mirror; his eyes her eyes in rearview; scraps; a hand on hers; her leg all beat up; the Corner Diner Café, order whatever you want, my brave girl; the wind, the sky, the storm; the sad parade of father figures who rotated in and out: Randy, Enrique, Dale…; none survived her mother long enough to be called Dad; she'd called him Dad; Dad kept tabs; no, Amon kept tabs; Amon, Randy, Enrique, Dale…She pounds the steering wheel, sobs, tries to scream, can't, as the wind-hail-rain-lightning-storm shakes the car like a mad thing. The storm's in full swing—wait! What if a tornado really is coming? For the first time since the storm began, she's afraid. Should she get out? Too late. The storm is too intense. She'll have to ride it out. The clock says 10:50. Guess she's missed the funeral.

Eventually, the wind subsides. The hail stops. The rain becomes a drizzle. The sky is no longer scraped and bruised. People trickle back to their cars. Her windshield is cracked in two places. No doubt her car is all dents and dings. She can't afford to fix it. Unless—"He left you something, dear," Heidi told her. She smiles. If it's money, she'll take it. If not—at least there was no tornado.

The Quarterly Issue 3 Fall 2015

How to Be

To try something (good lord, anything) else

Grow up, slowly and without noticing. Your mom is your best friend. Pick a school close to her. She will ask you to live at home. Shake your head, but cry when she drops you off on your first day. Call her the first night, in tears, and don't hang up until she asks if you'd like for her to come up the next day to have lunch with you. You're practically begging, pleading. Say yes, yes please.

Declare a zoology major because you think animals are cute and soft. You'd like excuses to touch them every day. Think you'd enjoy being a zookeeper. Working with lions and things like that. You stop crying. Call your mother every day anyway, by choice, without prompting from her. Call her in the mornings as you get dressed. Call her in between classes as you walk. She will learn all the names of your professors, your new friends, your social organizations, what you do every day in class.

In school, do poorly in Biology 101. Learn that it's hard to care about things like ectoplasm unless you're talking about the *X-Files* and struggle to understand cells that are so small you can't see them. Think it's not hard because you don't believe that they exist—you know that many of the realest things in the world are things you cannot see— but still, find it difficult to accept it when your professor says cells are living organisms. Think, Are they? Think, What is living? Think about how these cells do not laugh or cry or worry about what's for dinner. They don't pay the electric bill and they don't hate their exes and they aren't sad and lonely and loved and happy all at once. They exist, okay, but are they living? And are you *sure*, you ask your professor, are you absolutely *sure* these things are alive?

Fail biology. Get a dog, if you love animals so much.

Then go to page 41. You're a creative writing major.

The Quarterly Issue 5 Spring 2016

Absolution Bake Shop

As the family neared the compound, they caught their first glimpse of The Bakers. A dozen girls in long floral dresses with golden hair in elaborate braids walked along the side of the road. Each carried a woven basket covered with checked cloth, like the one Little Red Riding Hood brought to her grandma. Lydia looked at their homemade dresses and lace-up boots, then down at her own skinny jeans, halter top, and Adidas, and felt both jealous and sad for them at the same time.

The allure of the Bakers' treats was that they were all handmade by virgins. The girls baked all day at home, carried each batch up the hill to the store while they were still warm, and then their parents sold whatever was on hand to whomever was next on the endless line that stretched day and night from their cabin's front door down to the parking lot.

Lydia's brother Mitchell took his iPhone out of his jacket pocket and aimed it at the virgins, but their mother reached across the van seat and yanked it out of his hand. "No pictures!" she warned. "If you take their picture they won't serve us."

Obviously that rule didn't apply to the food. At rustic wooden picnic tables under shady blossoming trees around the compound, tourists aimed their phones at generously domed muffins, golden apple fritters, and cookies the size of dinner plates. There was also a good amount of trading going on. A piece of this for a taste of that. Everyone wanted to try everything.

The line to get in was about a hundred people long, and quite a few tourists toward the back were snacking on previous purchases while waiting for their next turn at the service counter. As the family inched gradually forward, music started drifting down the hill from inside the cabin. The melody sounded like a variation on the gospel children's song "This Little Light of Mine," but the lyrics had been changed, and the tone was much more pointed. "Jeeeeeeeeeee-sus is gonna drop a dime on you," a chorus of women sang. "Jeeeeeeeeeee-sus is gonna drop a dime on you. Jesus is gonna drop a dime on you, a dime on you, a dime on you, a dime on you."

"What does that mean?" Mitchell asked his parents. He was nervously fiddling with his phone, but he didn't take it out of his pocket.

"It's old-time slang from the time before cell phones," his father replied. "Pay phones used to cost a dime to make a call. So if you wanted to rat someone out to the cops, you'd use a pay phone and 'Drop a dime on them.'"

"But why would Jesus call the cops on you?" Mitchell asked.

"Maybe Jesus is gonna tell on you to God instead," Lydia suggested. They were all quiet after that until they reached the front of the line.

"Whoever has the money step to the register, the rest of your party can step to the side," came a booming voice up ahead. Lydia and Mitchell flattened their bodies against a wall of preserves in the entryway while their father stepped up to the counter.

Behind the cashier in a little food prep area, five round, sturdy women in aprons were decorating fresh-from-the-fryer doughnuts with glossy chocolate ganache, peanut-butter chips, and marshmallow fluff—each round morsel was an individual work of art. "Jeeeeeeeeeee-sus, is gonna drop a dime on you," the women sang as they worked.

"Forty dollars," the register woman said to their father.

"Forty dollars for what?" he asked, handing the money over anyway. His family certainly hadn't waited on that long line for nothing.

"Forty dollars for absolution," she replied, and thrust a wicker basket into his arms. "Next!"

Mitchell and Lydia didn't even wait to see what they'd gotten. They just turned around and raced each other back down the hill to the end of the line. Their parents peeked under the dishcloth on their way to join them, but their faces registered nothing.

"What did we get?" Mitchell shouted when his parents came within earshot. Their father handed their mother the basket.

"Pretzels!" she announced. Lydia and Mitchell stared at her in stunned silence. Lydia thought Mitchell might cry. Nobody reached for the basket.

"C'mon, these are good!" their father insisted, sounding angrier than he probably meant to. He reached into the basket, pulled out a big twist of dough, took a bite, and chewed for a long time.

"Look, they got pretzels," one young man whispered to another from the line forming behind the family.

"You have something to trade?" Lydia and Mitchell's father asked, eyeing their basket. They were going back for seconds, too.

"Sorry, no," the taller of the two replied. "It's just that they must really think you're a sinner in need of extra absolution. The Bakers know everyone is in line for sweets. So if they stick you with bread, it means you should come back and try again."

"I'm not made of money," Lydia and Mitchell's father grumbled to their mother. She gave her husband's arm an encouraging squeeze and they all stayed where they were on the line.

After a while, Lydia excused herself to search for a restroom. When she found the row of yellow and teal Porta-Johns out past the parking lot, the line for a stall was almost as long as the line for food. She waited as long as she possibly could, then gave up and jogged around to the far side of the cabin where there was a broad back porch, and beyond that, a heavily wooded area that looked private enough. On the porch, a dozen men and boys in coarse denim shirts and button-up pants with suspenders were moving busily like an ant colony, stacking long objects into piles. Lydia couldn't see what they were carrying clearly, since most of the piles were under tarps, but there seemed to be a lot of activity—counting, moving, arranging.

She was hustling for the tree line, but still straining to see what the men were doing, when she tripped on something heavy hidden in the grass. She stumbled and fell. She wondered for a moment why there was a small metal pineapple on the overgrown lawn. Then she noticed the handle with the metal ring on top. Then she screamed and wet her pants. The prickly warmth spread from the crotch of her jeans down both legs into her sneakers. The front of her pink shirt was soaked up to her bellybutton.

At the sound of her terrified yelp, a boy about Lydia's age leapt off the porch and came running. She was too scared to move, and also too embarrassed. But when he reached her, he just scooped up the grenade as if it were an apple recently fallen from the nearest tree, and helped Lydia to her feet. He pretended not to notice her stained clothes or the tell-tale smell, and offered her his arm to hold as they walked back toward the cabin.

"Why was there a grenade in the grass?" Lydia asked.

"We keep weapons hidden in different places, in case we need 'em," he answered. His Pennsylvania accent was thick and formal.

"Do you buy weapons with the money from the treats?" she asked.

"Yes ma'am," he replied, then steered her around another hidden grenade.

"What are they all for, though?" she asked. "The weapons. Why do you need so many?"

"Holy war," he answered. "It's coming. We just don't know when. In the meantime, the women are offering absolution to as many as they can."

"That's nice of them," Lydia said, though she wasn't really sure if it was.

"Wait here," he whispered, and left Lydia under the porch while he climbed the stairs. Above her head, she could hear boots moving swiftly back and forth and snippets of conversation. Rounds of ammunition were being inventoried and distributed. Occasionally someone would chuckle, but in general, the conversations sounded like they were strictly business.

The boy came back with a long flowered dress in his arms a few minutes later. It was off-white with small pink rosebuds all over it. The collar, long sleeves, and buttons down the front to the waist had clearly been hand-sewn with great care. "You and my sister look like you're about the same size," he said, handing it over. Lydia had never been so grateful or so humiliated. He turned his back politely and she slipped the dress over her head, and then she wriggled out of her wet clothes. When she was finished, the boy handed Lydia a burlap sack for her soiled clothes and cautioned her to stick to the path on her way back down the hill. Then he was gone.

As Lydia made her way back to the food line, a few tourists who had already eaten their fill and weren't afraid of getting kicked off the compound pulled out cell phones and took her picture. Even her own parents didn't recognize her until she was back beside them.

"Oh, honey!" Lydia's mother exclaimed. "Don't you look pretty!"

"Where'd you get that dress?" Mitchell demanded.

"I met a Baker and he gave it to me," Lydia said, hiding the sack of dirty clothes behind her back.

"See! I knew those pretzels didn't mean anything. They like our little girl the best," her mother said proudly, examining the stitching at the waist of the full, gathered skirt with her fingertips.

"We're done here," Lydia and Mitchell's father said firmly. "Get in the van."

The rest of the family waited a second to see if he was serious. He was. They all got back in the van, and once they'd made it onto paved roads again, Lydia and Mitchell sang a few rounds of "Jesus is gonna drop a dime on you," until they got bored with it.

Lydia stared out the window, fingering the delicate mother-of-pearl buttons now adorning her chest. She did a mental inventory of what flours and fruit they had at home. Satisfied their pantry contained all she'd need, Lydia decided that when they got back, she would try and make her family a pie.

The Quarterly Issue 3 Fall 2015

How to Be

With work

You have a cubicle on the third floor of an office building downtown. Your husband with golden eyes will insist he makes enough to support you both without the job. Explain to him you need this for reasons unrelated to money. Frame pictures of him for your desk. Call your mother from the work phone every day on your lunch break. Your new job requires you write copy for small-time companies you've never heard of. Write in rhyme. Write in couplets. Write in thirty seconds or less. Write sharply, like cheddar, and realize it's still cheese. But it's all the writing you will ever do again.

Your coworkers are kind. Share smiles and work gossip but leave the relationships in the office at 5 p.m. Dress business casual. Go home when the clock says to with nothing else to do. Leave work at work. Kiss the golden-eyed boy at the door when he gets home. Spend the evening with him. Sometimes he will bring home flowers just because. Go out to eat on Fridays. Thursdays go to his parents' house. On Tuesdays, make breakfast for dinner. Watch TV. Do puzzles. Laugh. Fight. Fuck. There will be kids one day, with freckles and sticky fingers and golden eyes like his. Not yet.

Invite your mother up for a visit to see the house. Make the five-hour trip home at least once a month for the first three, then every other month, then every four or five. Eventually just settle for going home over Christmas, at least. Pretend not to notice the envy in her voice when she asks after your mother-in-law, who lives five minutes away. She thinks she will be a stranger to her future grandkids.

Start to miss your academic days, when you didn't know the difference between work and life, passion and duty, when your peers—coworkers—were like friends were like family. You miss the blurred lines, personal is professional is personal, the business conversations at the parties, the drinks at the business meetings (like parties).

Decide to enroll in grad school and go to page 7. Before you do, kiss the golden-eyed boy goodbye.

Buttercup Chain

Willie pumped the arm of the Daisy BB gun and popped off a few random shots into the woods. She liked that it had a girl's name, Daisy. She liked the cold ping when she hit a coke bottle. She liked guns. When she was old enough, she'd buy her own. Dare had a .22 now and had pretty much left the Daisy for her, though he didn't outright say she could have it.

She continued on through the small paths she and Dare had made in the woods until she got to the ditch that bordered the woods and Sample's field. The corn wasn't tall yet but she decided to round the field and spy on the Sample farm anyway. When she got close enough, she noticed an old station wagon pulled up to the farm house. Old man Sample's family was visiting. She stalked around the edges of the property, moving from one tree to another, Daisy pulled up vertically beside her. She got close enough that she could've thrown a rock and hit the car when the sharp slap of the screen door and a wild commotion sent a panic through her. Her heart thudded so loud she could hear it.

But it was only Sample's grandkids who had burst out the door, with their mother's voice trailing after them, "Y'all stay in the side yard and don't you dare go in that barn or I'll skin you alive." There were three of them. The tallest was a girl but she was still just a kid, not nearly old as Willie. The two little ones appeared to be boys and were chasing and pushing each other, whooping and hollering. The girl had straw-colored hair and she wandered over past the small garden to where a clump of buttercups were growing.

She'll make a chain, Willie mentally jeered. The girl sat and began to do just that. Willie slipped back tree to tree, her heart racing, a plan forming as she circled around to where the girl was sitting. When she got as close as she could without coming out into the open, she whistled. The girl took no notice. Was she deaf or stupid or something?

"Hey you! Hey you stupid girl," Willie stage whispered to get the girl's attention.

When the girl turned her head around, Willie stuck her head and the barrel of the BB gun out from behind the tree. "Come on over here, girl," Willie commanded.

The girl looked confused but got up slowly, buttercup chain in hand, and came within three steps of the tree.

"Halt! Right there. Don't come no further," Willie commanded. "Sit back down and face the house."

The girl obeyed and Willie stared at her profile, considering what she meant to do.

"Who you?" the girl asked in a timid country voice.

"I'm your worst nightmare, that's who." That was a line Dare used on her and she thrilled now to be the one saying it.

"But what's your name?" The girl didn't seem to get it. She didn't seem to know enough to even be scared. She just sat there looking straight ahead at the farmhouse like she was in a trance. Maybe she wasn't quite right in the head.

"You see this here gun?"

"Can I look thataway now?"

"Yes. Look over here, then go back to looking at the house."

She turned and stared at Willie, then looked at the barrel of the BB gun. Her eyes were pale blue and her skin was sandy and freckled. Willie noticed how faded and thin her shirt was and thought it ought to be in the rag basket by now. The girl didn't seem at all nervous or scared like she should've been. She looked like someone walking in her sleep, sort of blank.

"You're my prisoner," Willie hissed.

When the girl didn't say anything, just kept looking vacantly at her, Willie kicked the tree. Then she pumped the gun a few times and shot into the clump of buttercups. The girl jumped and made a squeaky noise. That was more like it.

"You're going to do what I say, or I'm going to shoot you. You understand me, girl?"

"Yes, ma'am."

Willie might have thought she was being a smart aleck except her voice came out a little shaky and nervous. Still, the girl might be simple, calling her ma'am like she was a grown up. Willie decided to let it go.

"Now you come over here and give me that buttercup chain. Wait! First finish making it into a circle. Then come on over here and drop it by the tree." Willie didn't really want a buttercup chain but she was running out of ideas about what to do with her prisoner.

The girl did exactly what she was told and then went and sat back down in her former spot.

"What's your name?"

"Melinda, but everyone calls me Missy. I'm almost seven."

"*I'm almost seven*," Willie lisped, mocking her, even though she was beginning to feel a little bad about how mean she was being. "What you doing here, *Missy*?"

"Just visiting my granddaddy. Mama let us outside to play for awhile."

As if summoned, her mama appeared at the screen door calling out, "Y'all come on in now and say goodbye to granddaddy." The two boys started turning somersaults and cartwheels in the direction of the house. "Missy! Come on in," the mother yelled louder.

Missy turned to look at Willie and Willie hissed, "You're my prisoner. You don't go 'til I say you can go."

The panic in the girl's face both elated and shamed Willie.

"Missy Sinclair! You better get your scrawny hide over here right this minute." Her mother was coming down the steps in their direction.

"Not 'til I say so," Willie hissed again.

Missy plucked at the grass around her but stayed planted. When it was clear her mother was going to keep advancing on them, Willie said as calmly as she could, "Okay. You can go. But walk, don't run. Remember I got a gun on you."

Missy got up and walked toward her mother who was looking red in the face by now. When she got close enough her mother grabbed her by the shoulder and started shaking her hard.

"Girl, didn't you hear me calling you? You dragging your feet like dead lice 'bout to fall off you. What's got into you?"

"I couldn't move," Missy whimpered.

"What you mean you couldn't move?" her mother demanded.

"I was a prisoner. A mean girl back there was pointing a gun at me."

"What in Lord's name are you talking about?"

"That girl by the tree, she was pointing a gun at me and made me give her my buttercup necklace and said I was her prisoner and not to come when you called me," Missy hiccupped.

Her mother looked up and around. Willie held her breath and stayed behind the tree while considering making a dash for it. Then the woman hauled off and slapped Missy full on the face. The sharp sound stung Willie's ear.

"You better quit your foolishness, making up stories like that when you ain't minding. Lying tongues is straight from the devil. You keep that up and I'll tan your hide good, just see if I don't."

Missy was crying and hiccupping as her mother jerked her along by the arm toward the house, but she didn't say anything else about being a prisoner.

When the screen door slammed shut, Willie stayed frozen behind the tree looking down at the yellow chain near her feet. She inched it closer to her with the gun barrel and squatted slowly to pick it up. She stared at it before mashing it up in her hand and stuffing it in her pocket. No evidence, she thought. She backed up toward the trees behind her, careful to keep a trunk between herself and the house at all times. When she was back in the woods she continued to make her way quietly, even after she was long out of earshot of the farmhouse. But the sound of the slap kept ringing in her ears, pulsing louder and louder, becoming painful like the report of a rifle fired at close range.

"Buttercup Chain" originally appeared in *Third Wednesday*.

How to Be

With words

Be reckless. Give the stranger everything: words, promises, attention, adoration, secrets, sex. Recognize afterwards that he was always going to leave. Feel mature. Feel grown. Tell yourself it—he—the experience—something—was worth being broken. Don't tell your mother.

Take up smoking. Start drinking. Hide both from your parents. Ask what you could have done differently to make him stay. Change your answer more than you change your clothes. Hate him. Hate yourself. Don't answer your mother's calls.

Write like there's a gun to your head. Write like it will bring him back. Write like it will save your life.

The stranger will feel guilty now when he sees you but you must not mistake this guilt for affection, the way that you mistook his loneliness for love the first time. Do not relapse into hope, no matter how he sometimes smiles at you. He will start to say things like do you know I never meant to cause you pain? And you must always nod and say yes.

Realize that this does not make it okay, or better.

Your mother will wonder what has gotten into you.

To *a(void)* giving up and letting the whole world burn, jump to page 55.

There are no other options at this time. All you can do is keep writing.

The Quarterly Issue 6 Summer 2016

Author's Note

The theocracy of modern-day Iran continuously attempts to oppress and regulate social identity, resulting in cross-sections of the pious, defiant, condemned, and invisible. The concept of sexuality navigates these boundaries in frightening and sometimes disastrous ways. Because of strict Muslim Law and punishment, sexual relationships exist either within the confines of heterosexual marriage or in secret underground networks constantly in fear of discovery. More dangerous than the hidden world of heterosexual dating is the life of an Iranian homosexual. Iran's Theocracy does not tolerate homosexuality to any degree. The transsexual, however, can find a relatively safe, if not widely accepted, place in society. While homosexuality is a crime punishable by death, a transsexual is considered to have a health problem for which hormone treatment and sex reassignment surgery is an acceptable medical treatment.

The government subsidizes such surgeries and provides gender authentication paperwork to help assimilate individuals who have undergone treatment successfully. It is a booming business, and Iran is now second only to Thailand in the number of sex reassignment surgeries performed annually. This system arguably brings some relief for transsexual Iranians, but it creates a dangerous climate in which homosexual Iranians can be pressured into having surgery in order to position themselves in a societal structure that uniformly rejects and persecutes them.

The outcome is often tragic.

Wheat to Bread

Nothing absorbed death's scent. A shame, this one looked young. Bahar stroked the graying cheek. She traced a line down the shoulder, across the arm, along the wrist bone, detouring to the ring finger. A faint outline marked a removed wedding band. She imagined the girl's skin flushed, a beating heart pushing vessels open in response to her husband's touch. Bahar disliked the female body, too soft and forgiving, all curves where angles should be. She let go of the finger and spread the body's legs just a little. She pulled a puff of cotton and placed it over the hairy part, then gently closed things back.

There was a time, in Tehran, when all family members were allowed to wash and anoint their loved ones before they were lowered into the ground. But now, due to overpopulation and the laws of supply and demand, that privilege cost more than many could afford. So, most mourners made do spectating behind windows as bodies moved along the "prep for heaven" assembly line. She doubted the men's Wash House was a ridiculous as the women's, with all the wailing and chest beating. Just like a zoo, they lined up three or four thick to watch. Bahar wondered how many belonged to this one, blubbering and staining the glass she would eventually have to clean. Her finger moved along the leg, pushing into a fading bruise.

They'll lift your lifelessness and tumble you into a concrete tub for everyone to see, washing your delicacy away with cold water and lye. You won't gasp. Your skin won't bump at the cold. Those who loved you, those who envied you, even those who hated you will grieve for one dead so young, so beautiful. But when they see your toes curled in, your eyes open and clouding, your limbs flopping like a fish out of water, it's fear they push away. They know, we all know, that death will one day kiss our feet too.

"Stop playing with the body, freak." The supervisor stood close, breathing down her neck. "I didn't want to give you this job," she whispered. "But for your family name, I would have said no. Do you hear me?"

She started pulling the trolley away. Bahar straightened herself and squared her shoulders.

"This clay, so strong of heart, of sense so fine, Surely such clay is more than half divine—'Tis only fools speak evil of the clay, The very stars are made of clay like mine."

The supervisor stopped. "What did you say?"

"Nothing you would understand," Bahar answered.

The supervisor snorted and moved on. Likely she had never read anything but the Koran, much less heard of something as delicate as Khayyam's poetry. Bahar watched the body go, wishing for her own turn. She braced as they came one after the other for the next eight hours. Brush the hair, cover the indecent, on to the wash-room: her own private hell of nakedness and decay. Some fat, others old and frail, sometimes shaved where the cotton goes, or gray and patchy. Each body emptied of whatever animates, a silent sack of fingerprinted life decomposing. She had that in common with them. In this way she understood them best.

At the end of her shift, she shed her plastic clothing. She wrapped herself in a black Chador. Though not compelled to by law, Bahar pulled it up to cover her face. She would never be the stylish woman who wore a light scarf toward the back of her hair and tight fitting over-clothes. The more pious she seemed, the better for slipping under everyone's radar.

If she had the choice, she would stay indoors, always. But her husband wanted her to work, pay her own way. She feared it was because he planned to leave, abandon her, and his conscience would take it softer if she could stand on her own. She cried, a lot. But he just told her to look for a better job if she was unhappy and the subject was closed. He knew very well, for the likes of her, there was no better job.

Bahar clung to the thin layer of material shrouding her. She looked down and shoved through crowded women swaying like black seaweed in a strong current. Sometimes, when the thought of going home was too much, Bahar stood by the small opening at the far end of the Wash House. The finished product slid out, wrapped in beautiful white gauze, cocooned like the ancient mummies she'd read about as a child. Bahar wondered if death ended pain. Not just the hurt that crawled through her, shifting sides in her chest, racing around her stomach. She learned to live with that, and the strangeness of her body. It was the physical pain that haunted her.

She shook her thoughts away. She had no time for poetics today. It was his birthday.

Last year they didn't celebrate. She was recovering. Pink skin formed layers of new tissue as itchy cuts and stitches healed. The year before was the most perfect they had ever been. A time she chased in every thing she did. They baked a cake. A hideous inedible thing made from throwing flower and cracking eggs over each other's heads. But they laughed back then, and he touched her, leaving imprints of his lips on her flour-covered neck and chest. The batter sat congealing in a bowl while he made love to her on the kitchen floor, pushing and pulling at her with such a force that she secretly swore to give him anything.

The memories kept her from leaving. She constantly resurrected moments when time lapsed like water carelessly spilt. How they walked street markets, crowds of people a barrier for the electricity between them. Or the feel of him as they slept naked beneath sheets, she, afraid to move because he clung to her so tightly the slightest breath might wake him. Now she listened to the city stretch and yawn alone, in her own separate room.

When she stepped into the market. Agha Samir greeted her with a cold nod. She forced herself to meet his glare.

"Your cakes?"

He pointed to the section of the store she needed. There was a beautiful white one with fresh cream filling. He would love that. She chose a fruit tart instead. She paid, her Chador falling for a moment as she gathered her things. When she left, Bahar tried to ignore the young girl asking her mother what was wrong with the lady buying the cake.

Words lure so effortlessly. The holy men say there is no more sin in it than changing wheat to flour to bread. They make it sound so simple, dressed in clean pressed linen robes, meting out Allah's words. A parade of success stories and testimonials intended to leave no doubt. But you make up my mind for me with that beautiful voice. Don't you love me? How many times do you ask? And I, in my stupidity, forget to ask back. You swear so sweetly that you need me to be yours, legitimate, in the open. Now I wonder, were you the charmer or the snake?

Their flat was a beautiful three bedroom in the northern part of the city. Her husband made a profitable living as a lawyer and he came from a very rich family, not that they helped anymore. Bahar checked herself in the mirrored hallway. She tried to get her stringy hair under control, wiped the sweat off her face and repositioned her Chador. She unlocked the door and walked in. He was sitting on the couch, drinking beer from a bottle.

He glanced at her and looked away. She felt her ribs give against the sharp jab in her chest.

"I got you cake," she said.

Her voice sounded more excited than she meant as she lifted the box up. Her husband just sat, honey eyes focused on the TV playing Arabic music videos.

His guilt once comforted her. Now, she didn't even have that.

"Joonam, when do you expect her back?" a voice asked from the bathroom. "You know I don't like to be here when she gets home."

Bahar put the cake on the counter and moved into the kitchen, getting knives out to cut with. She ignored the spikes in her stomach, reaching up her spine, wrapping around her neck and prickling her cheeks with heat. She fought back tears as she got plates out with shaking hands.

The young man came out. When he saw Bahar he paused. She didn't need to look at him. She knew her husband's tastes. Perfectly amorphous, this one mastered the skinny jean and trendy tee. She could have worn the same thing before hormone therapy made her soft and plump. She wiped the infuriating tears streaming down her cheeks. He stood staring at her with bleached hair and sympathetic eyes. She hated him to the point of rage, but not for what he did, for what he had. He inched closer to her.

Disappear, right now, she willed.

"Shhhh," he whispered. "Don't."

She should have clawed his eyes out. She could smell her husband on him, not just the bitter scent of his ejaculate, but the musk of his passion. She drowned in envy. He put his hand on her shoulder and squeezed tight. She felt herself stir, grateful for any touch, and then she remembered the empty place, stripped of function, alien to any purpose. She felt useless, ugly, alone. And she had done it to herself.

Bahar began to cry again. The young man's arm wound around her.

"He loves you in his own way," he said.

It was a gentle thing to say.

"Come on, get yourself together. Let's try some of that cake."

She found the invitation repugnant but felt grateful for it. Damned or no, she would rather this than give him up. So Bahar cut the cake while the young man put plates on the table. Her husband smiled at him and wouldn't look at her. They ate and awkwardness gave way the more they drank. The young man served as a strange conduit. She felt him watching her. She shifted in her seat. What must he think of her? Disgust? Or even worse, pity? She couldn't meet his eyes. The moment passed, evaporating into the young man's chatter.

Her husband, never very good with alcohol, fell asleep on the couch. Bahar sat with the young man on the balcony finishing what was left of the cake. She looked at Mt. Tochal, its white peak towering over the city's dirty maze. Why couldn't she be that tall?

"It's guilt," the young man said.

"What?"

"The reason he doesn't touch you. He still loves you. Will always love you for what you did."

Bahar laughed. She drank the last of her beer.

"For in and out, above, about, below, 'Tis nothing but a Magic Shadow-show, Play'd in a Box whose Candle is the Sun, Round which we Phantom Figures come and go."

There was a long pause.

"Rumi?" the young man asked.

"Khayyam."

The young man nodded silently. "He told me you had the heart of a poet."

Bahar sighed. "He was never going to want a woman, was he?"

The young man laughed bitterly. "You think he wants me? He uses me to remember you."

They were broken shards of the same glass, and she was too tired to play "which piece is sharper." She stood up, wobbling a bit, and he reached out, putting his hands on her waist to steady her. The alcohol dulled her instinct to pull back. In a rush of courage she leaned down and kissed his lips. She pulled away before he could.

"Stay the night," she said. "I won't fight it anymore."

Bahar went back into the apartment, past her snoring husband, to her bedroom. She shed her layers, brushed her hair, slipped into an oversized T-shirt and spread her legs wide under the starched sheets. She wiggled her toes and waited for her mind to still, pushing away thoughts of the young man helping her husband to bed, undressing him, slipping in beside him. Their mattress would learn *his* body now, give to *his* contours. She couldn't cry any more. Her body chose sleep instead.

She woke to the sound of them making love. Bahar pulled her knees to her chest. Her small, distorted breasts pushed up against her and she felt rage pull back and surge into an uncontrollable wave. She screamed, loud, low, letting her old voice fill her chest.

Before she knew what she was doing, she was in the kitchen with a knife in her hand. She would have done it, cut them from her body, the breasts that weren't hers. She would have mutilated whatever parts of her still wanted him. But he stopped her. His strong arms grabbed her wrists, squeezed so hard she dropped the knife. She felt a strange calm as his body pushed against her. She shut her eyes and smiled, thinking he might hold her, or whisper something kind.

He let her go.

"I can't live like this anymore."

She realized she'd missed his tears. Seeing them now gave her a strange satisfaction. It was her last tie to him, and it would have to be severed. He read her thoughts just as perfectly as he once used to.

"You have to leave," he said.

Saveh was an expanse of sunflowers and pomegranate trees sprung from dust. Bahar hadn't been home in three years. Finally, at the end of a long two-hour drive they arrived at the family plantation. The gates were shut. Bahar got out and hit the intercom. She didn't recognize the static voice on the other end.

"Please open the gate," she said.

"Who is it?"

"Bahar."

"Who?"

"Halim agha's daughter," she said.

"But…"

Then she heard her father's voice in the background. "Open it! Open!"

As they made it down the winding drive, Bahar's stomach sank as she saw the servants lined in front of the house. She wasn't up for grand gestures, and these people would judge harsher than any other. The driver took her bag out for her.

"How much?" she asked.

"Ghabel," he answered.

Bahar sighed. "Please, how much."

"It's my pleasure."

"Please tell me what I owe you."

"90,000."

Everything in this damned country was a game of pretend. She wondered what would happen if she started saying okay when merchants bowed politely and refused to set a price for their services. Even at her wedding, Bahar had to go through the traditional pretense of saying "no" twice before accepting him. As if wanting something was shameful.

She gave the driver 95,000 Toman and one of the servants inched close to take her bag. Bahar felt the weight of raised eyebrows. She could almost hear the whispers forming in their minds. They would have a lot to talk about over their dinners.

"Pesaram," her farther said.

"Don't call me that," she said.

He was a short, stocky man. Since Bahar could remember, her father wore a varied version of the same brown suit every day, always a handkerchief in his pocket. Her father hugged her tight and for just a moment she let herself relax. She shut her eyes and his warmth seeped into her sagging body. She breathed deep, her arms at her sides, her cheek resting on his dusty lapel. A familiar scent of Paco Robanne mixed with earth slid through her.

"Your mother is in Tehran," her father said. "She will be sorry she missed you."

"No, she won't," Bahar answered.

She pulled away from her father and let him lead her into the house.

"Why didn't you tell me you were coming?"

"I didn't know," Bahar said.

"Is everything okay, Pesaram?"

Bahar fought back tears. "I said don't call me that."

Her father pat her on the back. "Let's have tea."

"Baba Joon, I need to rest."

Her father nodded, his eyebrows coming together in a bushy frown. "I keep your old room ready for you. But if you will be more comfortable in the new part of the house…"

The property at Saveh had been in their family for five hundred years. The original part of the house was small, with stunted rooms and plastered walls. Bahar's mother commissioned an architect from Tehran to build the new wing in a way that flowed seamlessly from the old, hiding air conditioning and satellite television beneath hand-crafted cobalt and turquoise tiles. Bahar found the modern wing sterile, empty of character. In her room, she heard aged whispers as sheer curtains flapped in the wind. She felt memories slide down the walls and wrap around her.

She shut her eyes, mostly to avoid the unchanged décor of wrestling trophies and soccer jerseys. Everyone had been so proud of her back then. She was strong and beautiful, with rosy cheeks and wiry muscles. She hid it as long as she could. But eventually, she gave in. A young boy that worked for her father kissed her, and in that moment, everything made sense. She no longer cared for Allah's word, or her family's shame. The force of her happiness when they were together erased all other costs. But they could not hide forever, and they were caught. Her father used his influence and their family name was left out of it.

The town stoned Majjid to death.

Allah forgive her, Bahar remembered every bloody break in his face.

I watched them do it. Did you know that? I didn't want you to be alone. I snuck away and hid in the shadows. Did you feel me there? The coward that let you die, that stood there while they bruised and battered you for something we both did, wanted. Your own family threw stones in hatred.

"Be happy for this moment, this moment is your life." I used to whisper that to you when you felt scared, worried they would find us. You never knew the words were Khayyam's not mine. And you believed me. What the hell did I know? I still hear your screaming. You were the brave one, even if by force. I have been in hiding since that day. And now I can't recognize myself. This is not my body. This is not my life. I should have let them stone me, too. That pain lasts only once.

"Pesaram, do you need anything?"

Bahar curled into herself. "Why do you call me that? I'm not your son anymore."

Her father came in and sat by her. "Look," he said.

Her father held a picture of seventeen year-old Bahram. He was just about to go to Tehran to clerk in a law office, hoping to get into law school. But he met his husband at the firm, and all other things faded. In the picture, he stood between his parents. His mother kissed his cheek and his father smiled for the camera. The sun fell on all of them in such a way it caught their happiness like a suspended dust particle.

"You will always be my son. I will always see the boy in this picture. Allah doesn't make mistakes, Pesaram. And whatever mistakes *you* have made by listening to foolish men, they can be undone. We can send you to Turkey, or Europe, even Amrika. The doctors there are very good."

Bahar felt calm for the first time in two years. Her father was right. It could be undone. But not with a trip to some other place, where doctors would cut and mutilate her again. Not with pretty words that lured her from the one thing she'd wanted since they killed that boy. It could not be undone by pretending anymore.

"You're right," she said. "Thank you."

Her father got up and smiled. "We will talk more when you've slept."

Bahar laid her Gender Certification Papers on the dresser next to the trophies. She wanted to take her wedding ring off, too, but it was too tight, and in truth, she hated to part with it. Who was she if not his? Instead, she took a piece of paper, put his name at the top and with trembling hands wrote.

I sent my Soul through the Invisible
Some letter of that After-life to spell:
And by and by my Soul return'd to me,
And answer'd: I Myself am Heav'n and Hell.

Would he match her tear stains with his own when he read it? Would he remember that he recited the poem over hot tea on a late night in the office? Could he even conjure up the young man whose eyes grew so wide with awe that someone else knew Khayyam by heart? She read the words again, laughing bitterly. Her stomach ached and her heart raced. Bahar ran her hands along her chest, down her sides, waiting for some pang of remorse. Not even her own body asked to be saved.

Nightfall

The sun is dead. They say the world will go completely dark in eight days. We believe them because the sky has gradually dimmed over the past few months. At first we didn't really notice. Then, slowly, it was perceptible. Some of us went to the doctor to have our eyes checked, wondering if we had developed glaucoma. Some of us drove around with our bright headlights on all day. I complained to Rosalyn that I was feeling cold all the time. We lived in Los Angeles and it was June. Rosalyn told me to put on a sweater. I slipped on an extra layer and all of this went on for several more weeks until all of our eyes checked out just fine and they told us what was happening.

The sun has run its course. We can stamp an expiration date on anything. Redwood tree: 2,000 years. Ladybug: 6 weeks. The relevant number associated with our sun is 4.5 billion years. Eight more days seems like a joke in comparison.

The sun will flicker and turn itself off. Or maybe it won't flicker. The light will just stop coming and it will just go black, like pulling a light bulb chain. Maybe it will explode and engulf us in light, like a bomb. I don't know. Maybe the scientists know. I think it will flicker, though, at least as a sort of warning. The thought of instantaneous darkness is unbearable to me. I am trying to get used to the idea of eternal nightfall.

Upon hearing the news about the sun, Rosalyn tells me she's been having an affair with our next-door neighbor, Héctor, a pleasant, middle-aged man from Chile who grows apples, tomatoes, and apricots in his backyard. During the ten years Rosalyn and I have lived in Laurel Canyon, he has handed handfuls of fresh produce over the fence, showering us with neighborliness.

"Him?" I ask, shaking with disbelief.

"Yes, I find him very attractive," Rosalyn says.

"Héctor?" I choke.

She sits quietly at the kitchen table, nodding, peering into her lap.

All I can think of are the apricot pies that Rosalyn made over the years with Héctor's apricots. Tarts. Muffins. Jars of jam. There are apricots sitting in the bowl on the kitchen table. I pick one up and roll it around in my hand, faintly fuzzy and soft.

I don't want to know how long it has been going on.

Rosalyn packs a bag and scoots out the door before I can say goodbye. Or *wait*. Which is what I really want to say. I say those things after the door slams and then I sit on our green parlor couch, numb for several hours, staring at an old black and white TV that isn't even on. The rabbit ears are uselessly askew.

The house is eerie-still until Tucker trots through the kitchen doggie door, his jangling tags busting the silence. He sits in front of me, unaware of Rosalyn's abrupt and heartbreaking exodus.

His golden tail whaps the floor.

"Looks like it's just you and me now, pal."

He cocks his head to the side, raises his flappy ears, and dutifully puts his head on my lap. I scratch the soft top of his head and mull over the possibilities.

Shutting off the alarm, stepping into the bathroom, like always, there is an unexpected sense of normalcy when I wake. In the shower I squirt the shampoo into my hand and it is every other Monday morning I ever had. This can't be true, though. I'll cry if I think about it any longer, so I don't think. I just scrub and rinse and stay in for nearly twelve minutes.

The whisk in the top right-hand drawer is missing and I suspect that Rosalyn pilfered random kitchen utensils as she scurried out the door. I scramble the eggs with a fork and wonder what else is missing.

The familiar thud of the newspaper landing on the porch never comes, so I toss a scoop of chow into Tucker's food bowl and head for work. He comes running at the clang and scarfs half of it before I even get out the door.

The highways are barren, weirdly traffic-less, abandoned strips of concrete that seemingly lead to nowhere. I turn on the radio. There is a jabbering panel of sun experts. The head of NASA is explaining what will happen to the earth after it goes dark. Plants will die. Animals will die. We will die, etc. I flip to another channel. They have a different panel of sun experts. The American Association for the Advancement of Science. The Nature Conservancy. The Ecological Society of America. I try a third channel. More experts.

I pull into the dusty lot and park in my usual spot, the lone car in a row of empty spaces. I walk toward the warehouse and Kevin approaches, his blue shirt tucked into his blue pants.

"You're late," he says.

I look at my watch. Ten minutes early.

"I'm just kiddin' ya. You're actually the only one who showed up today."

He punches me in the shoulder and exudes something between a laugh and a grunt.

"Where is everyone?" I ask.

"Guess they decided not to come to work because of the whole sun thing. I mean who needs ice cream if we're all gonna die?"

This strikes me as the ultimate theoretical conundrum.

I feel a little stupid for showing up today.

"Oh," I finally say.

"You're welcome to run your route. Safeway and Nelson's already called and said they're closing down. They are all out of food anyway. I guess you can hit Winston's and Galleria if you want."

I nod. It isn't as if I had other things to do. I've been delivering ice cream for almost twenty years. I am a man of routine.

After checking the stock and marking my inventory, I pull myself into my giant blue truck and lurch on down the road. I make the rounds faster than ever before. The joy of driving through near-empty highways in Los Angeles is something I've never known. The human-sized green leaves on the palm trees are beautiful for the first time. The buildings, all quiet now, mostly dark, stand like an empty movie set. There are a few people milling around, glancing up at the sky, and there is a couple sitting at a bus stop, waiting for a bus that will never come. Everyone on the road is more polite than usual, signaling lane changes, keeping to the speed limit, and nodding occasionally to the other drivers as if they were neighbors, not strangers.

A pair of gangly stock boys at Winston's pick up the usual haul of chocolate and vanilla. They tote pints of ice cream into the store, wandering in and out with baffled, mechanical sluggishness.

It isn't that we are scared or worried or sad. It's that we don't know how we are supposed to feel.

No one shows up at Galleria and I am left with a pile of undelivered ice cream in the back of my truck. In the middle of the asphalt parking lot, I climb into the back, pull a plastic spoon out of its plastic wrapper, and pop open a carton of peppermint. I lean against the cold metal wall and eat the entire thing. I miss Rosalyn.

The next morning, Kevin leaves a message letting me know that I needn't come into work anymore. I stand in the kitchen listening to his awkwardly paused farewell: "Hey, buddy. I guess you might as well stay home today. I'm going to close up shop here. Have a great da—uh, it's been nice working with you, I mean. I hope you have a— Well, take care."

I step into the backyard. Tucker runs around the yard, smelling, inspecting every corner as if something might have changed or moved or been altered behind his back. Dogs are always preoccupied with how things are and how they have been and if the two match up.

I glance over at Héctor's two-tree orchard. His place looks deserted. I pull a green apple from his tree and munch.

My own garden is a sorry rectangle of weeds. I allow them to live because they are like flowers, tricking me with their tiny white and yellow blooms. Their beauty has convinced me not to kill them, but season after season they just take over the entire yard, choking out my sunflowers and blue buttons.

I chuck the chewed apple core into Héctor's yard.

I lean over the other side of the fence, surprised to see my other neighbor sitting on her deck, camped out with a pile of books and papers around her. It isn't uncommon to find her in this exact position, but the neighborhood has mostly cleared out and I just figured I was the only one left.

I don't really know where everyone has gone. To be with their families. To be alone. I imagine them all flocking toward the beach for one giant party. Or hiding away in the tiny places they loved. I don't know. Maybe they are robbing banks and burning down churches. The stores have already been plucked empty, so there isn't much left to rob anyway.

I clear my throat.

She looks up, equally surprised to see me.

"Karl," is all she says, like she's questioning my actual existence.

"Hi, Atsuko."

We smile at each other in a way that is neighborly. But now every smile carries more weight than it did before.

"What are you doing here?" I ask.

"I'm working on this book."

Atsuko is a translator. She speaks seven languages. Her shelves are full of bilingual dictionaries.

Tucker jumps with his front feet on the fence, his head just barely able to see over.

"You should come over," she says. "I'll make you a cup of tea."

I nod and walk to the back gate. Tucker trots behind.

I am pleasantly satisfied to see that her backyard is in an equal state of disrepair, perhaps even slightly worse off than mine. Her grass, more reminiscent of hay, is almost up to my knees. Tucker joyfully searches for new things to smell, new things to dig.

"Have a seat, I'll be right back with some tea."

Atsuko runs into the house.

I survey the papers. Everything is in Japanese. I can't make out a thing.

We've been neighbors for a long time. We've always said hello over the fence, like neighbors do. We've commented on weather and yard conditions. I picked up Atsuko's mail when she was out of town. She took care of Tucker when we were out of town. We traded cookies at Christmas. Well, Rosalyn did. I stood there while they chatted, divulging a year's worth of information, grinning with shiny cookie plates in hand. Atsuko and I had tea together every so often, intermittently between weeks and months, and she was one of the few people whom I suppose I could call a friend.

She returns with a tray of tea. Green and white china. Cups the size of plums. A jar of honey with its tiny dipper.

The steam hovers when she pours it.

"Where's Rosalyn?"

"She left me."

"What?"

"She left me."

I don't really know how else to phrase it, or if I am supposed to give details.

"God, why?"

"She was having an—well, she and Héctor," I point across the yards—"were having an affair."

"Héctor?"

"Yeah."

"That's surprising. How strange."

I drip honey into the tea, and take a slow sip.

I thought of it as cruel and selfish. But maybe it is *strange*. It's all just strange.

"What book are you working on?" I ask.

Atsuko gathers up a few of the papers and organizes them into piles.

"It's called *The Boy Who Stole Souls*. It was written about a hundred years ago and no one has ever been able to translate it. They say it's untranslatable."

"Untranslatable?"

"Yeah, because there are so many concepts that don't exist in English. So many things that don't have an equivalent. If something doesn't exist in a language, you have to spend a lot of time describing it so that people can understand it," she says.

"So if it's untranslatable, why are you doing it?"

"I don't think anything is truly untranslatable. It just takes more time. More research. More attention to detail. More pages."

"What's it about?" I ask.

"It's hard to say for sure. Some people think it's about a boy who invents a machine that transfers souls from one person to another. Some people say it's about a boy who steals souls and keeps them for himself."

"What do you think?"

Atsuko laughed.

"I don't think it's about stealing souls at all. I think it's about making your own."

"What about the sun?" I ask.

I vaguely raise my hand to the sky, as if that explains it all.

It's like the word *sun* has taken on a new meaning. It has become interchangeable with a new set of words: end and death and dark.

Atsuko shrugs, "What about it? I've been working on this book for ten years, and it's almost done. I can't stop now."

I cradle my teacup in my palm. Tucker bounds onto the deck and collapses into a heap under the table. I sit while Atsuko continues to work, and she doesn't seem to mind the intrusion.

Over the next couple of days, my life starts to revolve around Tucker. Dogs live by routine, which is what I crave more than anything. We awake as the first pale light seeps into the window and take a long morning stroll every day. There are only a few days of light left and everything seems wilted.

As we circle the neighborhood, I determine that not everyone is gone. Some people are just holed up in their homes, like me. I run into the Browns who are also out for a morning walk and they say that they have been whiling away their evenings playing Scrabble. They kindly invite me to join them. I say sure, even though we all know that I won't come. It's too much of an imposition for me to intrude on their last days.

I see Greg half-bent over the hood of his Mini Cooper. He's been tinkering with that rusty old thing for years. The plates are small, white, British. A bottle of whiskey sits atop the roof of the car. He waves at me and pats Tucker on the head as we pass.

Jenny and Jenny, blonde-haired, same-named roommates at the end of the block are standing on ladders, painting their entire house red. I stand watching, curious. Jenny One climbs down and explains that red is said to bring good fortune. Jenny Two yells from the top of her ladder, "and fuck the neighborhood association."

Tucker and I mosey our way through the canyon.

The Krysinski Family is sitting on a blanket, just off the trail. Two moms and two boys sit in a circle eating muffins and orange juice.

The older boy asks if I want some breakfast.

I say I've already eaten.

The hills are already starting to lose color, fading to a dull tan. We track up storms of dust as we make our way around the canyon loop and head back. Tucker finds an especially appealing stick, carries it all the way home, and buries it in the backyard under the forsythia. I stop watering the yard, because there is no point in trying to keep the grass alive. The forsythia, usually bright yellow all summer, is pale and sagging. It will die soon, probably before the sun.

There is a brown paper package on the porch when we get home.

At the kitchen table, I tug gently on the tiny bow and the string splays itself across the table. The brown paper opens up and I slide it off to discover Atsuko's translation: a smooth stack of clean, white paper, dictionary-sized.

The pile of paper sits heavily in my lap as I flip each page over and rest it in an upside-down pile on the table next to my favorite chair. It takes me two days to finish. As I turn over the last page I sigh, a deep, full-lunged breath, my hands folded in my lap, I am filled with a kind of sadness. It is a sort of grief for everything we have yet to lose.

I continue to sit in my favorite chair, under a single lamp, and I watch the hovering moon through my window. Perhaps, we can learn to live under the moonlight. Maybe all of the plants and animals could simply adjust to function under moonlight. All the colors will turn to the deepest shades, and everything will feel like satin and smell like rain. Wouldn't that be lovely? It doesn't cross my mind until later that the moon won't glow without the sun.

I search Rosalyn's tidy desk. A stack of freshly sharpened pencils in a cup on the top. Bills filed away in card catalog drawers. I can only find one pad of paper. At the top is printed *From the Desk of Rosalyn Parker.* I look again for something else, but that's all there is. I scratch out *Rosalyn* and write *Karl.*

A note: *Atsuko—Thank you for the book. You're right, it seems it wasn't untranslatable after all! And how wonderful that you were able to finish it. Perhaps I could have you over to my place for tea next time?*

—Karl

I feel like a teenager, awkward and giddy, as I traipse across the moon-soaked lawn and stand on Atsuko's porch. I wonder if it is too late to ring the bell. I think that it is, though it is getting more and more difficult to tell time. I have no idea if anyone else is bothering to keep a regular schedule anymore. I slide the note into her mail slot.

I go home and wait. There are only two days left.

"Well, what did you think of the book?" she asks as I pour peppermint tea into tan mugs with etchings of mountain goats and buffalo. Rosalyn and I picked them up in Yellowstone National Park last year.

"It was one of the best things I've ever read," I say, immediately realizing my inability to articulate anything interesting about the book. I was never good at conversation.

"You really think so?"

"I do. It would have been a shame if it had been locked away from all of us non-Japanese speakers."

Atsuko smiles.

"I'm so glad I was able to read it," I add.

"You and I are the only ones."

"You haven't shared it with anyone else?"

"Who would I share it with? My editor has gone to San Francisco with her sister. My brother lives in Detroit. I can't send it to him. None of my friends are left."

We drink our tea and take comfort in the old habit.

My finger traces the outline of a buffalo. Where is Rosalyn? I don't know where she and Héctor have absconded to. I guess I should be glad of that.

"It seems unfair that you and I are the only ones who have been able to read this," I say.

Atsuko just sighs.

And then we come up with a plan.

We go to Atsuko's office, a small publishing company in West Hollywood. The door is locked, so Atsuko kicks in a window. She laughs as her booted foot goes through the glass and shards fall to the ground. Everything sounds so loud in the empty city. She climbs through the tiny hole and opens the door from the inside. I hold the giant stack of paper in the crook of my arm.

We find a copy machine in a dark hallway and stick the book into the manual feed. Atsuko loads the tray with paper and presses the button. Sheets fly through the machine and a replica is cranked out every three minutes.

We bundle the hot stacks of paper with giant clips and carry them out to my ice cream truck. We fill up the chilly compartment with piles of books.

We spend the whole day.

We dig through the recycling bin and salvage all of the useable paper.

We steal giant clips from other giant bundles of paper strewn about the office on desks and shelves, in binders and folders.

We use up every piece of paper in the entire office.

By the end of the afternoon, we've amassed a truck full of books, a refrigerated container of English translations.

I slide the truck door down with a clatter and flip the lock from left to right.

"Where should we go?" I ask.

"I don't know."

We hadn't planned that far ahead.

"I guess we'll just drive around."

So we drive. And we deliver.

We shove the book into mailboxes. We toss it onto porches. We feed it into slots. We slip it into open windows. We leave it on tables and chairs and bus stop benches. Sometimes we place it directly into the hands of an unsuspecting someone who just happens to be within arm's reach.

One book at a time we unload our cargo and it feels like tossing wads of money into crowds of people, only no one is there.

We drive around West Hollywood, Inglewood, Lakewood, Glendale. We make a giant circle, weaving through the neighborhoods, delivering our goods, bit by bit. One bundle at a time.

We end up back in Laurel Canyon and slowly hit every house on our street. I leave two copies with Jenny and Jenny.

By the time we make it back to our houses, the truck is empty. Success.

We sit on my porch steps, tired and leaning up against the side of the house.

Tucker roams around the front yard, his golden color starting to blend in with the dry grass.

"Do you think anyone will read it?" she asks.

"Sure."

I try to sound reassuring. I have no basis for what I am saying, but what does it matter? We'll never know either way.

"I'm sure they will. I'm sure someone will read it," I say more confidently.

Atsuko smiles and laughs a little.

Her laugh sounds the same way honey tastes.

We stretch out on the steps and wait for the sun to fade away.

Sunsets over Los Angeles have become slight and clear, not the deep murk that usually settles over the valley. I've become accustomed to those dark smears of color. I've watched so many sunsets from my porch; the industrial orange-pink that closed each day has become as familiar to me as Rosalyn's face, as Tucker's bark. As I watch the sun sink for the last time, I have the feeling that I will forget the old sun, that this last pale light, as strange and foreign as it seems to me now, is all I will remember of Los Angeles and everything that came before.

Contributors

SAMANTHA EDMONDS received her MA in creative writing from the University of Cincinnati in April 2017. She holds a BA in English from Miami University in Oxford, Ohio. Her work has previously appeared or is forthcoming in *Pleiades, The Indiana Review, Midwestern Gothic, Monkeybicycle, Phantom Drift*, and *McSweeney's Internet Tendency*, among others. She has a lot of pets. Find her on Twitter @sam_edmonds122.

KELLI JO FORD's fiction has appeared in publications such as *Virginia Quarterly Review, Forty Stories: New Writing from Harper Perennial*, and *New Delta Review*. She's been awarded a National Artist Fellowship by the Native Arts & Cultures Foundation, an Elizabeth George Foundation grant, and a Dobie Paisano Fellowship. She's a citizen of the Cherokee Nation and lives with her husband, Scott Weaver, and their daughter, Cypress, in Richmond, where she's working on a book of stories titled *Crooked Hallelujah*. You can find her online at kellijoford.com.

SADIE HOAGLAND has a PhD in fiction from the University of Utah where she worked as an editor for *Quarterly West*. She has an MA in Creative Writing from UC Davis. Her work has appeared or is forthcoming in *Slush Pile Magazine, The Black Herald, MOJO, Alice Blue Review, Oyez Review, Grist Journal, The South Dakota Review, Sakura Review*, and *Passages North*. She currently teaches Creative Writing at the University of Louisiana at Lafayette. More about her can be found at sadiehoagland.com.

RANDON BILLINGS NOBLE is an essayist. Her work has appeared in the Modern Love column of *The New York Times, The Georgia Review, The Rumpus, Brevity, Creative Nonfiction, Fourth*

Genre, and elsewhere. Her lyric essay chapbook *Devotional* is forthcoming from Red Bird in 2017, and the University of Nebraska Press will publish her full-length collection in 2019. A fellow at the Virginia Center for the Creative Arts and a resident at the Vermont Studio Center, she was named a 2013 Mid-Atlantic Arts Foundation Creative Fellow to attend a residency at The Millay Colony for the Arts. Currently she is a nonfiction editor at *r.kv.r.y quarterly*, Reviews Editor at *Tinderbox Poetry Journal*, and a reviewer for *The A.V. Club*.

KERRI PIERCE is a writer, translator, and mother living in Rochester, NY. She has translated works from seven different languages spanning several genres. Her short translations have appeared in places such as *Fiction* and *The New Yorker*, and her longer translations include novels and works of philosophy. She holds a PhD in Comparative Literature from Penn State.

EMILY REMS is a feminist writer, editor, rock star, playwright, and occasional plus-size model living in New York's East Village. Best known as managing editor of BUST Magazine and the co-host of BUST's podcast "Poptarts," Emily is also a music and film commentator for New York's NPR affiliate WNYC, and is the drummer for the horror-punk band the Grasshoppers. Her nonfiction writing has appeared in the anthologies *Cassette from my Ex* and *Zinester's Guide to NYC*, and her short stories have been published in *Rum Punch Press, Lumen, Prose 'N Cons Mystery Magazine, Writing Raw, PoemMemoirStory, The SFWP Quarterly,* and *The Borfski Press*. She was nominated for a Pushcart Prize for fiction in 2015 and is working on a novel. Follow her on Twitter @emilyrems.

N. R. ROBINSON grew up in Junior Village, a Washington D.C. government-run orphanage that was the largest institution of its kind in the United States. A ninth-grade high school dropout, he went on to earn a general equivalency diploma, graduate from the University of the District of Columbia, and work in corporate America. In 2006, N. R. left his executive position at Microsoft to begin the ten-year journey of scribing his coming-of-age memoir, *Our Family Walks*, from which "Our Institutions" is excerpted. He is a 2009 graduate of Florida Atlantic University's MFA in creative writing program, and a 2016 graduate of University of Missouri's PhD in English Literature program. N. R. is currently an Assistant Professor of English at Claflin University. He has been published in *Cactus Heart Press*, *The SFWP Journal* and *Quarterly*, *Bluestem Magazine*, and *New Ohio Review*. N. R. was a contributor at the 2015 and 2016 Bread Loaf Summer Writer's Conferences and the 2016 Tin House Summer Workshop. He can be found on Facebook at facebook.com/nickrobi.

JUNE SYLVESTER SARACENO is author of the poetry collections *Of Dirt and Tar* and *Altars of Ordinary Light*, and a chapbook of prose poems, *Mean Girl Trips*. Her work has appeared in various journals including *American Journal of Nursing*, *Southwestern American Literature*, *Steel Toe Review*, *Tar River Poetry*, *Worcester Review*, and others. She is a professor and English Program Chair at Sierra Nevada College, Lake Tahoe, where she teaches in the BFA and MFA programs. She is also founding editor of the *Sierra Nevada Review* and director of Writers in the Woods literary speaker series. For more information visit junesaraceno.com.

ATOSSA SHAFAIE received a BA in English literature from George Washington University and an MFA in creative writing from George Mason University. She was fiction editor for *So To Speak*, Publications Assistant at AWP, and senior editor for *Bartleby Snopes, A Literary Magazine*. She is currently the managing editor of the *UTC Journal*, a publication of the Utilities Technology Council. Her work has been published by *Scribes Valley*, *Dream Quest One*, *Coffee House*

Fiction, Fish, Savage Press, Winning Writers, The SFWP Quarterly,
and *Paycock Press*. Her fiction was also part of Call and Response, an
exhibit in George Mason's Fall for the Book Festival. Her flash fiction
earned honorable mention by *Glimmer Train*. She is currently working
on her first novel.

MORGAN SMITH is a former member of the Colorado House
of Representatives and Commissioner of Agriculture now living in
New Mexico and working as a freelance writer and photographer.
His major focus is on the Mexican border and his goal is to show that
there is another side to the violence we read so much about. He has
identified and writes about a number of individuals who provide aid to
the needy, often at significant risk to themselves. His articles appear in
a number of papers in Colorado, New Mexico, and Texas.

NANCY SMITH received her MFA in Writing from the University
of San Francisco and her MA in Media Studies from The New School.
Her work has been published in *Paper, The Rumpus, McSweeney's,
Compose, Seattle Weekly, Your Impossible Voice*, and elsewhere. She is
currently working on a PhD in Human-Computer Interaction at
Indiana University. More information can be found at her website,
somequietfuture.com.

KAYLEIGH WANZER is an English teacher in Boston. She
completed her graduate work at Binghamton University, where she was
also Managing Editor of *Harpur Palate*. You can follow her on Twitter
@heyirony.

About the Editor

MELANIE J. CORDOVA is the editor of SFWP Quarterly. She is the former editor-in-chief of *Harpur Palate* and assistant editor of the *Picayune*. She has a Ph.D. in English from SUNY Binghamton and works at Cornell University. She can be found on Twitter @mjcwrites.

Also from Santa Fe Writers Project

Magic for Unlucky Girls by A.A. Balaskovits

From carnivorous husbands to a bath of lemons to whirling basements that drive people mad, these stories are about the demons that lurk in the corners and the women who refuse to submit to them, instead fighting back—sometimes with their wit, sometimes with their beauty, and sometimes with shotguns in the dead of night.

"Balaskovits's anthology breathes fresh life into classic fairy tales. Readers who enjoy short fiction with a fantastical bent should pick up this award-winning book."
— Library Journal

Modern Manners for Your Inner Demons
by Tara Laskowski

Blending humor with a sharp social commentary, Laskowski introduces us to cynical yet sympathetic characters as each story unfolds. These characters are the folks you want sitting next to you at your next dinner party...or in your prison cell.

"Sly, clever, original take on the sad, bewildering, dead-on truths of being human."
— Kathy Fish, author of Wild Life

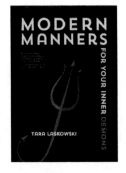

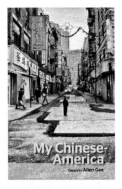

My Chinese America by Allen Gee

Eloquently written essays about aspects of Asian American life comprise this collection that looks at how Asian-Americans view themselves in light of America's O"Sly, clever, original take on the sad, bewildering, dead-on truths of being human."

"Intimate and wide-ranging, these probing essays complicate our picture of both Asian Americans and America."
— Gish Jen

About Santa Fe Writers Project

SFWP is an independent press founded in 1998 that embraces a mission of artistic preservation, recognizing exciting new authors, and bringing out of print work back to the shelves.

Find us on Facebook, Twitter @sfwp, and at www.sfwp.com